*The Black Book of Isobel Gowdie*

*And other Scottish Spells & charms*

*This Black Book*

*Belongs to:*

. . . . . . . . . . . . . . . . . . . . . . . . . . .

# The

# BLACK BOOK

## of

# ISOBEL GOWDIE

### And other Scottish

### Spells & charms

## Ash William Mills

### Scottish Cunning Ways

Edinburgh,

2021

# Issobel Gowdie

By

Ash William Mills

(26/05/2021)

*There wis a mickle carlin, her spells she cast in Auld hornie's name,*
*Issobell Gowdie wit she, an' Auldearn wis her hame!*
*Aull Bit a wee farmer's wivie, but a canny woman wis she tae,*
*Fae her charms didnae just call the divell (Devil), but with saints and the Fae!*

*Lang did she waulk her sorcerie, with her chairms an' magick verses,*
*Famed all a'rund, fae her cures and curses!*
*By manie she wis fear'd or respected, fae her power did possess'd,*
*Damned wis her faith, fae the divell's waulk she confess'd.*

*Of nichtly flytings frae Auldearne tae Downie Hills, she did stride,*
*In shape o' cat, craw an' hare, wit de deil at her side.*
*Aye, she did! Wit sorrow, sych an' mickle care, an' in de deil's name,*
*An' Wit elf-shott, chairm baggie an' dollie, manie did she lame!*

*But not always wis she wicked nor waulk'd sych devilish hairms,*
*Fae she healt de sick frae others witch's chairms,*
*she healt bairns frae bewitchment or had de quaking fevers,*
*Fae dis micht wis her dammed faith, frae fulks whom were deceivers!*

*Wit ever title suits thee; a witch, wese-woman or chairmer,*

*She'd wisnae just a wee wife o' a fairmer!*

*She'd stood 'oot fae the rest o' witches accused,*

*But wisnae set aside frae others kil't or abused.*


*Sa wit ever title suits thee, fae she wes a fine woman indeed,*

*H'er spirit ought tae be honour'd, wit dance, sung or hollow'd creed.*

*HORSE an' HATTOCK! Thus shout! an' now frae her enemies she gae an' flee,*

*fae she is a mickle wese-woman; An' her name is Issobell Gowdie!*

# ACKNOWLEDGMENTS

To my departed grandmother

## Esther White

Firstly, I must thank my ancestors and familiar spirits who has been divine spark and driving force in seeking out their long-forgotten practices. To my mum **Maureen Mills** and my Aunty **Jean Webb**, the two strongest women in my family I know! But to mostly, a BIG thank to good friends for their constant encouragement in writing this book and always pointing me in the right direction, especially to **Angie Simmons** (Wild Rose), **George (Hares) Bowling** and **Richard Haycock** who I class as my witchy family. A big thank you also goes to **Kalden Mercury** (*The Crooked Path: An Introduction to Traditional Witchcraft*) who helped me with proofreading and the editorial process. For **Rafael Espadine** and **Johnny Decker Miller** for contributing their beautiful artwork to this book. My gratitude goes to such authors as **Emma Wilby, Graham King, A. D. Mercer** and **Joyce Froome** for their great work and the inspiration of this book. To **Derek Simpson** at *Old Book for Curious Witches* for sharing interesting pieces on folklore, magic and witchcraft from his personal book collection which I have used some of that material in this book. Finally, but not lastly, to the team at the **School of Scottish Studies, The University of Edinburgh library**, and the **National Libraries of Scotland** for not only taking great care of the brilliant tomes they possess but for their help in obtaining and searching out the folkloric material needed for the content of this book.

# TABLE OF CONTENTS

"The First Encounter" – Isobel Gowdie, acrylic on canvas panel by Rafael
Espadine

"The painting portrays a Scottish woman accused of witchcraft, Isobel Gowdie, having her first encounter with the Lord of the witches (you know who) for the first time, as she described it happened when she once walked in the fields. At the back, the famous Dunnottar castle - which is situated near that area - can be seen.

Was the encounter physical or was it a vision? The painting poses that question by showing a split image in a dreamy perspective that shows a suggestion of Isobel's chambers where a candle silently burns in the night while she is also seen in the fields in plain daylight...

The truth might be incredibly sad. According to researchers, Isobel could have been raped, abused, probably starved constantly and maybe even suffered from ergotism, a disease that causes hallucinations. But also, according to historians, the visions Isobel reported have a deep shamanistic content, too much to be just the fruit of a highly imaginative peasant. Especially the content on fairy lore, which was not exactly what judges were expecting it would be and may hold the key to older magical traditions of that area."

**-Rafael Espadine, 2020**

# FOREWORD

By Graham King, previous curator of the Museum of Witchcraft and magic and author of *The British Book of Spells and Charms*

As I write this, I have a well-thumbed copy of McPherson's 'Primitive beliefs in the North-East of Scotland' sitting on my desk. I was, therefore delighted to hear that Ash William Mills was writing this volume about the spells and charms of Isobel Gowdie who is, herself, now an important part of Scottish Folklore.

Gowdie's involvement in witchcraft and her 1662 confessions have always been controversial and so much important information surrounding her remains a mystery. But the poetic beauty and enchanting nature of her charms cannot be disputed. Many song writers and authors have been inspired by these confessions including Robert Graves who reconstructed her famous shape shifting charm into a song in The White Goddess. I once married this charm to the Scottish folk tune Twa Corbies for the album 'Songs of Witchcraft and Magic' published by The Museum of Witchcraft in Boscastle.

The fact that Gowdie continues to intrigue and influence writers, folklorists and artists is to be celebrated and I sincerely hope that her magic and the inspired work of Ash William Mills will charm readers for many years to come.

*Cantil o, Cantil ee!*

*Joy to all thee gone before*

*Whose longer stay had pleased us*

*Cantil o, Cantil ee!*

*Joy to all thee left behind*

*Whose leaving would have grieved us.*

*Cantil o, Cantil ee!*

*Joy to all thee still to come*

*Whose song may lift the weary.*

*Cantil o, Cantil ee!*


*(From The Road to the Isles*, Macleod, 1927)

Graham King 2021


"In *The Black Book of Isobel Gowdie*, Ash William Mills masterfully crafts a tome of Scottish spells and charms. Rooted in the ever evocative lore of Isobel Gowdie, this book provides readers with an in-depth look at the craft of Scottish witches, magicians, and cunning-folk. Reflecting Mills's deep love for his homeland, *The Black of Isobel Gowdie* is a bewitching read filled with mystical curiosities and wonders of days past."

Kelden, author of *The Crooked Path: An Introduction to Traditional Witchcraft* and *The Witches' Sabbath: An Exploration of History, Folklore, and Modern Practice*

# INTRODUCTION

Britain has a long rich history in witchcraft, magical traditions, and magical practitioners known as charmers, fortune-tellers, Wise Women/Men, or Cunning Folk, and Scotland is no exception. Scotland is immersed in magic and the supernatural, and the characters of witches and magicians are at the backbone of the folktales and folk-belief within Scotland. Scotland is inhabited by people from many different cultures of the past, each contributing to this beautiful mixing cauldron of Scottish folk magic practiced still to this day. This magic spreads across our lands from all different directions, and this is apparent in the languages spoken in Scotland, with *Spae* (Norse) coming from the far northern islands and highlands, *draodhachd (Gàidhlig)* from the west, and the *airtes* or *magik* (Anglican) in the lowlands and borders. Even in the area where Isobel Gowdie resided in the northeast was most reputed with magical folks as the Wizard Michael Scot, mystical societies as the Horseman's/Miller's word and warlocks so powerful that they matched their cunning with the devil's- and won! This may be the reason why still today these regions are known as the Warlocks Country. In the past, everyone practiced folk magic in one form or another which was passed onto from mother to son or father to daughter, much of which was passed on contra-sexually through oral tradition. It is not until the 19th and 20th centuries, when folk beliefs and practices were slowly declining, that folklorists began to record them in writing. No matter how ignorant or romanised their approaches were, we must give gratitude to these early folklorists for at least preserving a lot of folk traditions in Scotland. Other than the early modern trial records, a lot of the spells, charms and magical operations mentioned in this book has been reproduced from other reputable books written by folklorist of the 18th and 19th centuries which detail the magical folk practices of Scotland. Folklorists such as Martin Martin (*Description of the Western Isles of Scotland,*1703), Alexander Carmichael *(Carmina Gadelica*, 1891-1900), John Gregorson Campbell (*Witchcraft and the Second Sight in the Highlands and Islands of Scotland*, 1902), and F. Marion McNeill (*The Silver Bough*, 1957) have

15

contributed to the work involved in preserving Scotland's magical folk tradition and belief, and indeed to this book also. For me, it is by digging into these old dusty books, long forgotten, that the magic of our ancestors can be revived, re-purposed, and even modernized to suit present-day circumstances. Doing so allows a new breath of life to be given to Scotland's rich heritage of magical traditions. In recent years, I have been shocked at the level of some modern folklorists or magical practitioners publishing in their book's material of Scottish content in its standard English translations of charms and spells only and not providing the Scots, Doric, Orcadian, or Gàidhlig they were originally recorded or relayed. A book that comes to mind is the publication of *Carmina Gadelica* by Floris Books (Edinburgh, 1992) which, as much as it is a complete work of Alexander Carmichael, is purely directed towards the English-speaking reader only. I always find this as both problematic and naïve of the modern writer as it only contributes to past ignorant institutions which do not fit today's values in cultural awareness and positive promotion. So, although I have provided a standard English translation, being a supporter of the use of local dialects and minority languages, I have provided certain material in this book as they were originally recorded. Both the speaking of Scots and Gàidhlig have a long history of persecution and ridicule in Scotland which is sadly still experienced in some communities but thankfully, the use of these languages is protected and supported legally by Language acts set by the Scottish Parliament.

Isobel Gowdie, the "Queen of the Scottish Witches" as she has been referred to today, as well as her magical repertoire and detailed accounts in her confessions have been a massive inspiration to many recent artists and even been the backbone of some modern witchcraft practices today. Artwork, songs, plays, and other projects have been the centre point in recent centuries, although I feel she has been speaking through others in the Scottish collective-unconscious for centuries. Most recently, there has been the ground-breaking book *The Visions of Isobel Gowdie* by Emma Wilby, the amazing music album *Isobel Gowdie* (2013) by Ex Reverie band, the exhibition 'Betwixt and Between: Isobel Gowdie, The Witch of Auldearn (2019)' at the Museum of Witchcraft and Magic, and many more, including a wee online event organised by myself in celebrating Isobel Gowdie on the anniversary of her last confession via my Instagram channel. She has also served as the inspiration for the writing of this book of Scottish spells and charms as well as for the contributing artists.

For some years now I have worked on a book that was not only a reflection of modern Scottish folk magic but also packed with spells, charms, and magical rites which were practiced in Scotland's Cunning past. When I was not spending my time studying Scottish History and Ethnology at the University of Edinburgh, I spent it at the School of Scottish Studies and the Survey of Scottish Witchcraft searching through trial records, folkloric content, and folktales of Scotland associated with witchcraft, Cunning Folk, and folk magic. I was massively inspired by books such as *The British Book of Spells and Charms* by Graham King, *The wicked shall decay: charms, spells, and Witchcraft of Old Britain* by A. D. Mercer which are both complied with spells and charms from the historical accounts of witchcraft and trial records, and material collected from the early folklorists of the 19th and 20th centuries. Originally, when I first started writing this book, I intended for it to just be a compendium of folk magic, spells, and charms worked by the Wise Men and Women of Scotland. But the more I continued to research and contribute to the material, the more that this book took on a life of its own. It was not until I was more than halfway through finishing, that the book's true character came to light.

It was around the time of the anniversary of Isobel Gowdie's confessions that I had a vision of her come to me in a dream. I decided to do a live event in honour of Isobel Gowdie on Instagram, and it was then that the penny dropped! At the time I already had a large chapter entitled "The Black book of Isobel Gowdie" due to the massive amount of magical content Isobel supplied in her confessions of 1662. It then dawned on me, that not only did I want to supply a book of Scottish spells and charms of the past, which could be still workable today as I originally intended, but now I was inspired by Joyce Froomes *Spell Book of the Good Witch of Pendle* which is an imagining of what a spell book belonging to Janet Device might have been like if such a book had ever existed.

17

So, with the great number of spells, charms, and magical actions that Isobel Gowdie gave orally to her inquisitors it would have been worthy of a small book of charms if she had one in her possession. However, there are several possible reasons why she did not submit her charms to the written word. Firstly, Scotland had a long-standing reputation of oral tradition where tales, traditions, antidotes, and charms/spells were passed on by word of mouth from one member of their kin to another. Secondly, many working-class people were illiterate during the early modern period of Scotland with exception of wealthy, "educated" classes of society who were fortunate to have studied at a university. Thirdly, but most importantly, is that such a book was dangerous to have in a person's possession and if found by the clergy or authorities would be sure evidence for prosecuted under acts which prohibit "*any maner of Witchcraftis, Sorsarie (sorcery) or Necromancie*" which often included being sentenced to death. Some of the charms that Isobel testified to, had diabolical elements of *maleficia*, or harmful magic, and invoking in the Devil's name which I add, was not an uncommon practice regarding involving demons, or "devils" in conjurations found in magic books such as *The Black Books of Elverum*.

This book is intended for the modern magical practitioner who is looking to utilise a bit of Scottish Cunning craft into their practice, or for those just looking to contribute towards their collections as a keen folklorist, anthropologist, or historian of all things magical. Whatever is your intention, I hope it helps give you a glimpse into Isobel Gowdie's social conflictions, spiritual beliefs, and her life as a magical practitioner. So now, come sit yourself by the hearth fire, grab yourself a wee hot toddy and listen as Isobel Gowdie teaches you the charms and spells from her repertoire and those from the other wise men and women from around Scotland.

# ISOBEL GOWDIE AND JENET BRAIDHEAD'S CONFESSIONS.

## 13th April- 27TH May 1662

### *As Translated by Eddie Murray* (2005)

AT AULDERNE [1], [*in the parish church*] the thirteenth day of April,
1662. IN PRESENCE OF MASTER HARRY FORBES, Minister of
the Gospel at Aulderne; WILLIAM DALLAS of Cantray, Sheriff
Depute of the Sheriffdom of Nairn; THOMAS DUNBAR of
Grange; ALEXANDER BRODIE the Younger of Lethen;
ALEXANDER DUNBAR of BOATH; JAMES DUNBAR,
appeirant thereof: HENRY HAY of Brightmoney; HUGH HAY of
Newtown; WILLIAM DUNBAR of Clune; and DAVID SMITH and
JOHN WIER in Auldearn; WITNESSES TO THE CONFESSION
after specified, spoken forth from the mouth of ISOBEL GOWDIE,
spouse of John Gilbert, in Lochloy. [2]

The which day, in presence of me JOHN INNES, Notary Public,
and the abovenamed witnesses, all undersubscribed, the said
ISOBEL GOWDIE, appearing penitent for her heinous sins of
Witchcraft, and that she had been overlong in that service, without
any compulsion proceeded in her CONFESSIONS in the following
manner, to wit:

'How did you meet the Devil?

'As I was going between the farmsteads of Drumdewin and the
Heads I met the Devil, and there made a sort of covenant with him –
I promised to meet him during the night here in the Kirk [*church*] of
Aulderne, which I did.'

'What happened?'

'The first thing I did that night was deny my baptism. Then I put one of my hands on the crown of my head and the other to the sole of my foot and renounced all between my two hands to the Devil. He was in the reader's desk with a black book in his hand. Margaret Brodie from Aulderne held me up to the Devil to be baptised by him. And he marked me in the shoulder and sucked out my blood from the mark and spat it into his hand, and, sprinkling it on my head, said, "I baptise thee Janet, in my own name!"'

'And then?'

'After a while we all left.'

'Where did you next meet the Devil?'

'Next time I met him was in the New Wards of Inshoch.' [*an old ruined 'castle' or keep near the farm where she lived with her husband.*]

'And what happened at that meeting?'

'He had sex with me.'

'How did the Devil appear to you?'

'He was a big, dark, hairy man, very cold – I found his come as cold within me as spring well-water. Sometimes he had boots and sometimes shoes on his feet – but his feet were always forked and cloven. Sometimes he would be with us as a deer or a roe.'

'Tell us about the things you did in his name.'

'John Taylor and his wife Janet Broadhead from Belnakeith, [*blank*] Douglas and myself all met in the churchyard in Nairn and raised an unchristened child from its grave. And at the end of Breadley's cornfield, just opposite the Milne of Nairn, we took the child and clippings from our finger and toe nails and wee drops of all sorts of grain and some kale leaves, and hacked them all up into little pieces and mixed them together. We put a part of it among the dung heaps on Breadley's land. That way we took away the fruit of his corn and all, and we shared it amongst two of our covens. When we steal corn at Lammas we take only about two sheaves when the corn is ripe, or two stalks of kale, or thereabouts and that gives us the fruit of the cornfield or kaleyard where they grew. And it might be we'll keep it until Yule or Easter and then divide it amongst us.'

'How many are you?'

'There are thirteen persons in my coven.'

'And where do you meet?'

'The last time our coven met we and another coven were dancing in the Earlseat Hills. The time before that we met between Moyness and Boghole, and before that we met beyond the Meikle Burn. The other coven was in the Downie Hills so we went over to join them, and met up near the houses at the Wood-end of Inshoch.

'Then?'

'After a while we all went home.'

'When did you meet after that?'

'Before Candlemas we met east of Kinloss, and there we yoked a puddock-plough. The Devil held the plough and John Young from Mebelstown, our Officer, drew it.'

'Tell us about this "puddock-plough".'                    [*'puddock'* = *frog*]

'Puddocks drew the plough, like oxen. The traces were made of dog grass. Its coulter was made from a half-gelded ram's horn and a bit of horn was used as its blade. We went around two or three times with all of us in the coven going all the while up and down with the plough, praying to the Devil for the fruit of that land, and that thistles and briars might grow there.'

'What else does your coven get up to?'

'When we sneak in to any house, we steal food and drink and we fill up the barrels with our own piss again. We put besoms in bed beside our husbands until we return to them again. We were in the Earl of Moray's house in Darnaway [*Darnaway Palace*]. We got plenty there, and ate and drank only the best, and took some away with us.'

'How did you get in?'

'We went in at the windows.'

'What else will you confess?'

'I had a little horse and I would say "Horse and Hattock, in the Devil's name!" And then we would fly away, wherever we would, like straw flying about on the highway. We can fly like straw when we want – grass straw and corn stalks are like horses to us. We just put them between our feet and say "Horse and Hattock, in the Devil's name!" If anyone sees the straw in a whirlwind and doesn't bless himself we can shoot them dead if we want. Anyone shot by us, their soul goes to Heaven but their bodies stay with us – they will fly to us like horses as small as straws.'

'Anything else?'

'I was in the Downie Hills and was dined there by the Queen of Faerie – more food than I could eat. The Queen of Faerie is finely clothed in white linens and brown and white clothes {etc}. The King of Faerie is a fine-looking man, well built and broad faced... {etc.} ...[3] and there were elf-bulls rollicking and roistering up and down and they scared me.

'When we take away any cow's milk we pull hairs from the tail and twine it and plait it the wrong way in the Devil's name, and then we draw this handmade tether between the cow's hind feet and out between its forefeet, in the Devil's name, and that way we take the cow's milk with us. We take sheep's milk too. The way to take or give the milk back again, is to cut that tether.

'When we take away the strength from anyone's ale and give it to someone else, we take a little drop from each barrel or stand of ale and put it in a jug in the Devil's name. And in his name, with our own hands we mix it into the other person's ale and this gives her all the strength and body and goodness of her neighbour's ale. To prevent us getting the ale it should be well blessed – then we have no power over it.'

'From where do you get this power?'

'We get all our power from the Devil. When we ask him for it we call him "our Lord."'"

'And what else can you do with this power?'

'John Taylor and his wife Janet Broadhead from Belnakeith, Bessie Wilson from Aulderne, Margaret Wilson who's married to Donald Callam in Aulderne, and myself made a clay image to kill the Laird o' Park's male children. John Taylor brought the clay home in a fold of his plaid and his wife broke it up very small, like meal. She sifted it in a sieve and poured water into it, in the Devil's name, and kneaded it hard until it looked like rye dough, and made an image of the Laird's sons. It had all the parts and features of a child – head, eyes, nose, hands, feet, mouth and little lips. It wanted none of a child's features, and its hands were folded down by its sides. Its texture was like a crab or a scraped and scalded piglet.

'We put its face near the fire until it shrivelled with the heat, then we put it amongst the hot embers until it glowed red like a coal. After that we would roast it now and then; every other day a part of it would be well roasted. All the Laird's male children will suffer by it if it isn't found and broken, as well as those who've been born and died already. It was still being put in and out of the fire in the Devil's name. It was hung up on a peg. It's still there in John Taylor's house, and has a clay cradle around it.'

'Who knew about this image?'

'Only John Taylor and his wife Janet Broadhead, Bessie and Margaret Wilson and Margaret Brodie, all from Aulderne, and myself – we were the only ones there when it was made. But every one of the witches in all the covens learned of it at the next meeting after it was made. And all those witches as yet untaken still have their own power – and now they also have the power that was ours before we were taken. [4] Now I have no power at all.'
'Who are these witches as yet untaken?'

'Margaret Kyllie from [..........] is one of the other coven. Meslie Hirdall who's married to Alexander Ross in Lonhead is one of them. She has a fiery complexion. Isobel Nichol from Lochley is one of my coven. Alexander Elder from Earlseat and Janet Finlay his wife are in my coven. Margaret Hasbein from Moyness is one. So are Margaret Brodie, Bessie and Margaret Wilson from Aulderne and Jean Marten and John Mathew's wife, Elspeth Nishie. They all belong to my coven. The Jean Marten I mentioned is Maiden of our coven and John Young from Mebestown is its Officer.

'Anything else?'

'One time, Elspet Chisolm and Isobel More from Aulderne, Margaret Brodie [..........] and I got into Alexander Cumming's dye-house in Aulderne. I got in in the shape of a jackdaw and Elspet Chisolm was in the shape of a cat. Isobel More was a hare, and Maggie Brodie a cat, and [...........] We took a thread of each colour of yarn in Alexander Cumming's dying vats and tied three knots on each strand in the Devil's name, and stirred them about in the vat, widdershins. That way we completely took away the strength from the dyes and made sure they would only dye black, the colour of the Devil in whose name we stole the strength of the right colours that were in the vats.'

All of which premises, so spoken and willingly confessed and declared forth from the mouth of the said Isobel, in and by all things as above set down, I, the said John Innes, Notary Public, have written as here presented; and with the said witnesses above named, in further testimony and witnessing of the premises to be of verity, we have underwrit the same with our hands: day, year and place above specified.

*following:]*                    [*Signed by the*                    John Innes,
                                 Notary Public.

25

MR HARRY FORBES, Minister of Aulderne, Attests.   W.
DALLAS of Cantray, Sheriff-Depute, Attests.


A. BRODIE, witness to the said confessions.          HENRY
ROSE, Minister at Nairn, Attests the foresaid


HUGH HAY of Newtown, Attests.
Declaration, as to the principal substantials.


W. SUTHERLAND of Kinsterie, Attests these
GEORGE FINNIE in Kirkmichael, attests.


Confessions.                                         JOHN
WEIR in Aulderne, attests.

### *NOTES TO ISOBEL'S FIRST CONFESSION*

1.    *A little village a mile or two outside the Moray Firth fishertown of
Nairn, twenty miles east of Inverness. The origin of its name is shrouded in mystery.
The later Scots-speaking inhabitants would hear its name differently from the Gaels
who also still inhabited the area. In Scots 'auld' means old and some referred to it as
Auld or Old Erin, meaning Old Ireland (at that time Scottish Gaelic was still called
'Irish.') But in Gaelic 'alt' means 'the stream of.' It is the second part of the village
name that is still debated – alt eirann, the stream of the Irish? Alt Eren, the stream of
the Goddess? (according to a notice at a village bus stop.) The modern spelling is
Auldearn, but for the purposes of publishing them in* Legacy *I will stick to the
spelling as used in the original Confessions – Aulderne.*

2.    *In the listed names of witnesses 'of' means that person was a landowner,
e.g. 'William Dallas of Cantray', whereas 'in' means they did not own land, e.g. 'John
Weir in Aulderne.'*

3.    3.    *In a footnote to the official record's 'etc.' Robert Pitcairn said: 'It is
a thousand pities the learned Examinators have so piously declined indulging the world
with the detailed description of these illustrious personages. Under the singularly
descriptive powers of Isobel Gowdie, much might have been learned of* FAIRY-
LAND *and its Mythology.'*

4.    4.    *One thing is immediately apparent from Isobel's first confession –
she* didn't *give herself up, as every future commentator would claim. 'All those witches
as yet untaken,' she says, and then '…before* we *were taken.' Isobel was 'taken' –
captured or arrested – and she was not alone, hence the plural. Next day another
witch, Janet Broadhead, or 'Breadheid" in the local Scots dialect, confessed at a
different venue not far from Aulderne.*

## THE CONFESSION OF JANET BROADHEAD.

AT INSHOCH, the fourteenth day of April, 1662. In the presence of PATRICK DUNBAR of Balnaferry, Sheriff Principal of the Sheriffdom of Elgin and Forres; HUGH HAY from Newtown; ARCHIBALD DUNBAR from Meikle Penick; ARCHIBALD DUNBAR from Lochloy; WALTER CHALMER from Balnaferry; JAMES COWPER from Inshoch; JOHN WEIR in Auldearn; and a great multitude of all sorts of other persons; WITNESSES TO THE CONFESSIONS AND DECLARATION set down hereafter, spoken forth from the mouth of JANET BROADHEAD, spouse to John Taylor in Belnakeith.

The which day, in presence of me JOHN INNES, Notary Public, and Witnesses abovenamed and undersubscribed, the said JANET BROADHEAD, professing repentance for her former sins of Witchcraft, and that she had been overlong in the same service, without any pressure proceeded as follows, to wit:

'FIRSTLY, I knew nothing about witchcraft until I married John Taylor. It was him and his mother Elspeth Nishie who enticed me into that craft.

'And the first thing that we did was we made some druggeries from dog's flesh and mutton to use against John Hay from the Muir. It took away his crops and killed his horses, cattle, sheep and other farmstock. Then we spread it outside his house to kill *him*, and he died soon after.'

'So you were involved in this killing?'

27

'No. Only my mother-in-law and husband. They did it to teach me. That was my first lesson from them, (etc). When they got me to consent to the craft they took me to the Kirk of Nairn one night. And the Devil was in the Reader's desk with a black book in his hand.'

'Who was at that meeting?'

'At that meeting there were Bessie and Margaret Wilson from Aulderne, Margaret Brodie, Barbara Friece, Helen Inglis, Janet Burnet, Elsbeth MacBeith, Elspeth Nishie and Barbara Taylor. Bessie Hay was there, and Archibald Man with his daughter Marjorie Man, and Elspeth MacHomie, Bessie Friece and Isobel Friece, Agnes Torrie and Elspet Chisolm.

'Alexander Elder from Earlseat was there with his wife Janet Finlay. Elspet Laird from Milton of Moyness was there. So were John Robertson from Leithen and his wife Grisaille Sinclair, and Alexander Shepherd from Milton of Moyness with his wife Janet Man; Marjorie Dunbar from Brightmoney, [blank] Kyllie from Wester Kinstrae and Alexander Leddie from the same place.

'Elspet Gilbert from Leathenbar was at that meeting, and Agnes Brodie from Leathen, Janet Smith from Arry, Bessie Peterkin from Torrich and Alexander Bell from Drumdewin. He's a charmer. Isobel Nichol from Lochley was there, and Bessie Young, Elspet Falconer, Margaret Hutchens and Walter Leddy. They were all there that night. And my husband John Taylor, who was Officer then, though John Young's the Officer of my coven now.'

'What happened at that meeting?'

'After I arrived there the Devil read their names from the book and my husband John Taylor, who was Officer then, stood at the

Kirk door and repeated the names as they were read out. They came in as their names were called. Bessie Wilson from Aulderne sat next to the Devil and Bessie Hay sat on his other side. Janet Burnet sat next to her and Espeth Nishie sat next to her mother Bessie Wilson. She was Maiden to her mother's coven. All the others came in and sat down as their names were called.'

'What happened then?'

'The Devil had sex with them all, all over the place. Then he called my name, and my husband presented me and he and Margaret Wilson from Aulderne held me up to the Devil to be baptised. I had to put one hand on the sole of my foot and the other on top of my head, renounce my Kirk baptism, and give everything between my hands to the Devil. Then he marked me on the shoulder and sucked blood from the cut with his mouth. He spat it into his hand and sprinkled it on my head, and baptised me "Christian" in his own name.'

'And then?'

'Right after that everyone went home to their houses.'

'When did you next see the Devil?'

'One morning a few days later he came to my house when my husband was out ploughing. He said he wanted to examine the mark he had given me. Then he took me to bed and had sex with me, and gave me a coin like a seftain [?]'

'How did he appear to you?'

'He was a big dark and hairy man, and very cold. When he came in me it felt like spring well-water. He promised to see me again within eight days, and he did and had sex with me again and gave me another bit of money like the first, but they both turned red and I got nothing for them. After that he would visit me regularly every three weeks or so and have sex with me.'

'When did your coven next meet?'

'We next met in Darnaway Palace and drank and feasted there. Then we would meet every ten, twelve or twenty days. When we had our Great Meetings, Walter Leddy from Pennick, my husband John Taylor, and Alexander Elder were in charge of proceedings, after the Devil. But at the smaller meetings myself, Jean Sutherland (who's dead now), Bessie Hay, Bessie Wilson and Janet Burnet would be in charge [......................................................] we took Drumdewin's corn and shared it amongst ourselves.'

'What else?'

'We would shoot cattle as they pulled the plough.'

'Anything else?'

'Agnes Grant who was burnt [*as a witch*] on the [*blank*] hill of [*blank*] was hired by Elspet Monro to destroy the Lairds o 'Park and Lochloy and their succession. Me and my husband along with Elspeth Nishie and Bessie and Margaret Wilson from Aulderne convened with the Devil in Elspeth Nishie's house. We took dog's flesh and mutton and chopped it up fine with an axe, then boiled it in a pot of water the whole forenoon. I took it out of the pot and the Devil put it in a sheep's bag [*stomach*], still mixing it up with his own hands. We were all on our knees before him with our hair about our faces and our hands raised up, looking steadfastly at the Devil,

30

praying to him, repeating the words he had taught us that would kill and destroy the Lairds o' Park and Lochloy and their sons and succession.

'That night we went to Lochloy and skittered the mixture all over the gates and round about them and on other places the Lairds and their sons would likely frequent. Then we changed into crows and stood about the gates and in the trees opposite. It was so done that if any of them touched the mixture or stood on it, it would strike them with boils and kill them. Which it did, and they died soon after.'

'Why were they to be killed?'

'We did it to make their house heirless — it would harm no one but them. It was Kathren Souter, who was burnt [*as a witch*] that shot William Hay, the Laird o' Park's brother. But it was that bag that killed the last two Lairds o' Park.'

'Anything else?'

'Four years ago me and my husband along with Isobel Gowdie and Bessie and Margaret Wilson from Aulderne made a clay image of the Laird 'o Park's eldest son. My husband brought the clay home in a corner of his plaid. It was made in my house with the Devil himself present. We broke the clay up into meal-sized pieces and sifted it in a sieve and mixed it with water I brought home from the Rood Well in an earthenware jar, repeating the words the Devil had taught us, saying them in his name as we mixed it. Then we were all on our knees with our hair about our faces and our hands raised to the Devil, staring at him as we repeated the words three times he had taught us to destroy the Laird's sons and make the House heirless.'

'What did this image look like?'

31

'It was very roughly made, like rye-dough. It was about the size of a seadge [*an edible seaweed*] or a crab and had all the features of a boy – head, face, eyes, nose, mouth, lips and all – and its hands were folded by its sides. It was put near the fire till it dried and wrinkled and then we placed in hot coals till it was hard. Then we took it out of the fire and wrapped it in a cloth and hid it away on a shelf or sometimes under a chest. Every day we would wet it then roast and bake it, and every second day we would turn it at the fire, until the bairn [*child*] died. Then we hid it away and didn't touch it again until the next bairn was born. Within six months of that bairn being born we took the clay image from its cradle and cloth and every now and then we'd dip it in water and – like we did to the first one that died – every other day we'd bake it and roast it at the fire until the new bairn died too.'

## ISOBEL GOWDIE'S SECOND CONFESSION.

At Aulderne, the third day of May, 1662, about the hours of two or three in the afternoon or thereabouts: IN presence of MASTER HARRY FORBES, etc. [1]

The which day, in presence of me, John Innes, Notary Public, and witnesses, all undersubscribed, the said ISOBEL GOWDIE, professing repentance etc. [2]

'After that we would only sometimes meet as a coven – sometimes more, sometimes less. But a Grand Meeting would be held about the end of each Quarter. There are thirteen people in my coven, and each one of us has a spirit to wait upon us, when we please to call on him.

'I don't remember all the spirit's names, but there is one called SWEIN who waits upon Margaret Wilson from Auldearn. He's always dressed in grass-green and the said Margaret Wilson has a nickname, PICKLE NEAREST THE WIND.

'The next spirit is called RORIE who waits upon Bessie Wilson from Auldearn. He's always clothed in yellow. Her nickname is THROUGH THE CORNYARD, [..........................]

'The third spirit is called THE ROARING LION, who waits upon Isobel Nichol from Lochlow. He's always dressed in sea-green. Her nickname is BESSIE RULE.

'The fourth spirit is called MAC HECTOR, who waits upon Jean Marten, daughter of Margaret Wilson. He's a young-looking devil, dressed always in grass-green. Jean Marten is Maiden to the coven I am in, and her nickname is OVER THE DYKE WITH IT because the Devil always takes the Maiden in his hand, beside him, when we dance gillatrypes and when he leapt from [.....................]  he and she would say "Over the dyke with it!"

'The name of the fifth spirit is ROBERT THE RULE and he is always dressed in faded dun. He seems to be in command of the rest of the spirits, and he waits upon Margaret Brodie from Auldearn.

'The sixth spirit is called THIEF OF HELL WAIT UPON HERSELF, and he also waits on Bessie Wilson.

**'THE SEVENTH SPIRIT IS CALLED THE RED REIVER AND HE'S MY PERSONAL SPIRIT . HE WAITS UPON ME AND IS ALWAYS DRESSED IN BLACK.**

'The eighth spirit is called ROBERT THE JACKS, always clothed in dun and seems old. He's a glaikit, goukit spirit! [3]  And the woman's nickname that he waits on is ABLE AND STOUT. [4]

'The ninth spirit is called LAING and the woman's nickname he waits on is BESSIE BOLD. [5]

'The tenth spirit is named THOMAS A FAERIE etc. [6] There would be many other devils waiting upon our Master Devil, but he is bigger and more awful than the rest of the devils, and they all reverence him. I would know them all, one by one, each from the other when they appeared like a man

'When we raise the wind we take a rag of cloth and wet it in water. And we take a laundry stick and knock the rag on a stane, and we say three times:

'I knock this rag upon this stane,                    *stane = stone*

To raise the wind in the Devil's name –

It shall not lie until I please again!'

'When we wanted to lay the wind, we would dry the rag and say three times:

'We lay the wind in the Devil's name

It shall not rise 'til we like to raise it again!'

'And if the wind does not instantly lie after we say this we call upon our spirit, and say to him:

'THIEF! THIEF! Conjure the wind, and cause it to lie'

'We have no power over rain, but we can raise the wind when we please. —— He made us believe [.....................] that there was no God before him.

'As for elf arrowheads, the Devil shapes them with his own hand, and then delivers them to Elf-boys, who shape and trim them with a sharp thing like a packing needle. When I was in Elfland I saw them shaping and making them. When I was in the Elves' house, they

34

would have very [..................] them making and shaping. And the Devil gives them to us, each of us gets so many, when [...................] Those that make them are little folk, hollow [*barrel-chested?*] and hunchbacked. They speak gruffly, like. When the Devil gives the bolts to us, he says:

'Shoot these in my name,

And they'll not go whole hame.'                    [*whole* = *unharmed*]

'And when we shoot these arrows, we say:

'I shoot that man in the Devil's name,

He shall not whole win hame.

And this shall be also true –

Not a bit of him shall be on lieu.'               [*on lieu* = *on life, alive*]

'We have no bow to shoot with, but spang them from off our thumbnails. Sometimes we'll miss. But if they touch, be it beast or man or woman, it will kill them, even if they had a coat of mail on them.

'When we go into hare-shape we say:

'I shall go into a hare,

With sorrow and sigh, and meikle care                    [*meikle*
= *great*]

                           And I shall go in the Devil's name

      ,                          Aye while I come home
again.'                  [*Aye while = and stay until*]


'And instantly we start into a hare. And when we want to be out of that shape, we would say:

'Hare, hare, God send thee care!

I am in hare-shape just now –

But I'll be in woman-shape right now.'

'When we want to turn into the likeness of a cat, we say thrice over:

'I shall turn into a cat,

With sorrow and sigh, and a black shot!

And I shall turn in the Devil's name,

36

Aye while I come home again.'

'And if we want to turn into a crow, we say three times:

'I shall turn into a crow,

With sorrow and sigh – and a black throw!

And I'll go in the Devil's name,

Aye while I come again.'

'And when we want out of these shapes, we say:

'Cat, cat (or crow, crow), God send thee black shot (or black throw),

I was a cat (or crow) just now

*But I'll be in woman-shape right now.*

           Cat, cat (or crow, crow) God send thee a black shot! (or a black throw!)'

'If we, when we're in the shape of a cat, a crow, a hare or any other likeness, go to any our neighbours' houses, being Witches we will say:

'I conjure thee, Go with me!'

'And they instantly turn into what we are, either cats, hares, crows, etc., and go with us wherever we want

'When we wanted to ride, we'd take windle straws or beanstalks and put them between our feet, and say three times:

'Horse and hattock, horse and go,

'Horse and pellatis, ho! ho!'

'And immediately we fly away wherever we want. And lest our husbands should find us out of beds, we put a besom or a three-legged stool in beside them, and say three times:

'I lay down this besom, in the Devil's name —

Let it not stir until I come home again!'

'And it immediately seems like a woman, beside our husbands.

'We cannot turn into the likeness of [a dove or a lamb?] [7]
'When my husband sold cattle I used to put a swallow's feather in the beast's hide, and say three times:

'I send out this beef in the Devil's name,

May much silver and good price come hame.'

'I did the same whenever I sent out a horse, cattle, webs of cloth or any other thing to be sold, and always put this feather in and said the same words three times over, to make the commodities sell well,

etc. [...................................................................] three
times:

'Our Lord to the hunting he is gone,

[........................] marble stone,

He sent word to Saint Knitt [...................]

'When we want to heal any wound or broken limb, we say three
times:

[...........................................................................]

[...........................................................................]

He put the blood to the blood, till all upstood,

The lith to the lith, till all took with;

Our Lady charmed her dearly Son, with her teeth and her tongue,

And her ten fingers –

In the name of the Father, the Son, and the Holy Ghost!' [8]
'We say this three times, stroking the wound, and it gets better.
For the boneshaw [ = *sciatica*] or pain in the haunch: "We are three
maidens charming for the boneshaw, by man of Middle-earth, blue
beaver, land fever, all manner of sickness – the Lord scared the Fiend
with his holy candles and yard foot stone! There the pain is, there it's
gone! Let her never come again!"'

'For fevers way say three times: "I forbid the quaking fevers, the sea-fevers, the land-fevers and all the fevers that ever God ordained, out of the head, out of the heart, out of the back, out of the sides, out of the kidneys, out of the thighs, from the points of the fingers to the nibs the toes – out shall all the fevers go. In Saint Peter's name, Saint Paul's name, and all the saints of Heaven. In the name of the Father, the Son and the Holy Ghost!"'

'And when we took the fruit of the fish from the fishermen, we went to the shore, before the boat came in, and on the shoreside we would say three times:

'The fishers are gone to sea,

And they'll bring home fish to me.

They'll bring them home inside the boat –

But they'll only get the smaller sort!'

'So we either steal a fish, or buy a fish, or get a fish from them for nothing, one or more. And with that we have the fruit of the entire catch in the boat, and the fish the fishermen are left with are just froth, etc.

[At this point there is sea change in Isobel's statements. Perhaps the Calvinist Commissioners got tired of listening to their confessing witch recite Catholic folk-cures. Their interest was in the witch as destroyer, not healer, and possibly Isobel was moved on to more interesting topics.)

'The first voyage [*sic*] that I ever went on with the rest of our covens was to Ploughlands, and there we shot a man between the plough shafts and he instantly fell to the ground on his nose and mouth. And then the Devil gave me an arrow and made me shoot a woman in those fields, which I did, and she fell down dead.

'In winter 1660 when Mr Harry Forbes, the Aulderne minister, was sick, we made a bag of the galls, flesh and guts of toads, some barley, finger- and toenail clippings, the liver of a hare, and bits of cloth. We mixed it all together and steeped it overnight in water, all minced together. And when we put it in the water Satan was with us and he learned us the following words, to say three times over. They go like this:

'He is lying in his bed – he is lying sick and sore,

Let him lie in his bed two months and three days more!

Let him lie in his bed – let him lie in it sick and sore

Let him lie in his bed two months and three days more!

He shall lie in his bed, he'll lie in it sick and sore,

He shall lie in his bed two months and three days more!'

'When we had learned all the words from the Devil, as I said, we all fell down upon our knees with our hair down over our shoulders and eyes, and our hands lifted up, with our eyes fixed steadfastly upon the Devil, and said the words correctly, three times, against Mr Harry Forbes' recovering from his sickness.

'During the night we crept into Mr Forbes bedroom, where he lay, with our hands all smeared [with the mixture out of the bag?] to

41

swing it over Mr Harry as he lay sick in his bed. And during the day we sent one of our number, who was most familiar and intimate with him, to wring or swing the bag upon Mr Harry, as we had not succeeded during the night; and this was done.

'If any of [the witches] comes into your house, or are set to do you evil, they will look strange – like, misshapen, [.....................] dishevelled, with their clothes sticking out. [9]

'The Maiden of our coven, Jean Marten, was [...............................................] We do nothing important without our Maiden.

'If a child be bewitched, we take the cradle [... and a looped belt and put the cradle ...] through it three times, and then put a dog through it. The we shake the belt above the fire, and then throw it down on the ground until a dog or cat walks over it, so that the sickness will come on the dog or cat.'

All of which was spoken through the mouth of the said ISOBEL GOWDIE, etc. [10]

**Eddie Murray 2005**

*But Isobel Gowdie of Lochloy still had much more to say, and another two confessions to make. It would be her third confession that would make her famous – or infamous – after Pitcairn's work was published. It was a full account of the huge-membered Devil and the orgies they enjoyed with him, of magical flights and trips to the Faery Otherworld, and detailed accounts of murders from on high with the elf bolts, of the feasts and the break-ins and the horseback rides across the night sky to the quarterly Great Meetings… and much more*

## NOTES ON ISOBEL'S SECOND CONFESSION

1.   1.   'As in preceding Deposition' (Pitcairn.)

2.   **2.**   'The same preamble is repeated, with the account of her baptism and carnal dealing, etc.' (Pitcairn.)

3.   **3.**   'A glaikit gowkit spirit' = a stupid-looking vacuous spirit.

4.   **4.**   Viz. Bessie Hay.

5.   **5.**   Viz. Elspet Nishie

6.   **6.**   'Isobel, as usual, appears to have been stopped short here by her interrogators when she touched on such matters.' (Pitcairn.) Yet 70 to 100 years earlier (the Scottish Act against Witchcraft was made statute in 1563) this was exactly the information that the witch hunters were after. Before the 1591 North Berwick case and James' Demonology it was for consorting with the Faery that Scottish witches burned. After the North Berwick case the Devil goes striding across the fiery pages of the Scottish Witch hunts. Evidently by the year of Isobel's confessions, 1662, the Calvinist commissioners were not the least bit interested in admissions of consorting with the Faery. In the early recorded Scottish cases the psychomp initiator of witches tends to be an elderly, grey- or white-haired man. After Demonology he becomes a mature swarthy man – as if in the wake of James' Demonology the indigenous 'druid' had been replaced by an imported but eventually Scots-speaking 'chovohano.'

7.   **7.**   'There is a tradition in Morayshire that Witches could not appear in the shape of a dove or lamb.' (Pitcairn, footnote.)

8.   **8.**   Pitcairn remarks dryly: 'It appears very singular to us who live in the Nineteenth Century, that Satan should have taught his servants to invoke the Saints, and even the Holy Trinity. The charms recited by his disciples are usually fragments of ancient monkish rhymes; and most of them were such as many good Roman Catholics of the lower orders, even in these times, would not scruple to use, for the supposed cure of their bodily ailments.'

9.   **9.**   Interestingly a Channel Islands witch called Collette du Mont confessed in 1617 to attending a sabbat and that 'There were fifteen or sixteen other witches there, but she could not recognise them at first, because they were blackened and disfigured.' (Nigel Cawthorne, Witchhunt.)

10.   **10.** 'The same form and subscriptions as in the preceding confession [of Isobel Gowdie], with the Notorial Attestation etc. of John Innes.' (Pitcairn.)

43

# ISOBEL GOWDIE'S MAGICAL WORLD

Isobel Gowdie, known as the "Witch of Auldearn" was the wife to a farmer named John Gilbert. The two lived in a "Fermtoun" in Lochloy, Nairnshire. Gowdie was brought forward, along with others such as Janet Braidhead, to the Kirk of Auldearn under charged of Witchcraft and Sorcery in 1662. She made four detailed confessions between 13th April and 27th May, apparently without the use of torture. These confessions have made a lasting impression on both historians and folklorists due to the richness of Magical charms, witches, and fairy lore in her confessions. Isobel's confessions have been remarked to have been the most exceptional testimony given by any witchcraft suspect in British history. We know nothing of events leading up to Isobel's confessions or even what happened to her afterward. We can only assume, given her testimony, that she was found guilty and taken by cart outside of Nairn to Gallowhill. Here she would have been made to show public repentance before being strangled and burnt. Anyone interested in a more in-depth investigation into Isobel Gowdie's life and history, I would highly recommend Emma Wilby's book *The Visions of Isobel Gowdie* which I have used myself as the main source of information in this section of the book. So, I owe massive gratitude to Emma Wilby for her extensive research and great insight into Isobel's life!

Isobel's world was surrounded by magic, with folk beliefs and practices involving fairies, witches, and the devil. The *Fermtoun*, or farm town, was a small farm hamlet in an area named Lochloy. With only a collection of cottages for agricultural workers, Lochloy was set a good few miles away from the nearest parish of Auldearn. Being set apart from the parish of Auldearn, Isobel and her own communities' social life would have been quite different from that of the parish. The communities of Lochloy and Auldearn hardly interacted, with their only interactions being that of trading goods or attending church. Even then, although permitted, many people did not attend church as often as they were expected to. It's likely that with the busy working life Isobel and her kin would have led, she would not have attended church regularly. In fact, during my time studying at university I have heard of cases where often women's daily tasks would have been so overwhelming, they would have urinated themselves between tasks. Putting that aside, Isobel would have been subjected to several magical ideas and activities through her time as a farmer's wife as well as from the community of a *Fermtoun*. Magical practices such as averting cattle of witchery or the evil eye, curing cattle with simple popish charms, or help sell beef at the market as mentioned in her confessions were common among rural farming communities. She would have been familiar with the magical idea of the *Toradh* or substance of field or cattle- milk, butter, and cheese, referred to in her charms of taking the 'fruit' of fishes or the field. She most likely witnessed many seasonal folk traditions such as the gathering of the last sheaf of corn; termed the '*maiden*', if an early harvest, or a '*carlin*', a late one. Another agricultural practice that may have been known to Isobel was the Gudeman's Croft (or the Devil's Plantation as it was known in England), a small piece of land intentionally left uncultivated for the "Gudeman", chief of the fairies, or the devil in order that he would not spite the crops elsewhere. Fairy creatures known as the *bodachan sabhaill*, or "the little old man of the corn, were paid with great reverence by the farmer throughout the northern areas of Scotland, for they helped to thresh the corn, made up straw bundles, and saw that everything was kept in order.

Those magical practices may have been common in the general populace is also evidenced by Isobel's curing charms such as those for bewitched children, fevers, broken bones, etc that such magical practice might have been in the general populace. Also, in wee communities like Isobel's, there was little distinction between charms and prayers, and they often went hand-in-hand in the world of working-class people. From Isabel's confessions, we know that her husband was from the cattle-rarer classes of agriculture society, so it was very possible that she spent the winter months at home with her husband and cattle. The other half of the year she would likely have not seen much of her husband who would have taken their cattle in summer shielings. Although she may have been busy with child-rearing or other tasks (which her trial records do not go into detail about), she would have been left to her own devices during these months. During a time when society was male-dominated, perhaps Isobel found freedom and individuality in the early summer months denoted in confessions would denote the early summer months. Again, it was during this time, without the interference of men, that Isobel and her other female companions were left to discover their own personal and spiritual expressions.

One thing we know, is that before the time of her confessions she certainly wouldn't have referred to herself as a "witch" given the social and religious views of her time. As Emma Wilby points out, her life as a farmer's wife would have been "so laborious that there would have been little opportunity for a woman like Isobel to do anything with their hours such as to *coeven* or gather at a witches' sabbath. However, she may have been a wise women or simple charmer given that 60% of her 23 recorded charms are Christian in content, involving the names of Saints, Holy Trinity, and most of all, Jesus Christ! Most of her charms seem to be quite genuine and contain elements like others recorded in early modern Scotland. For example, compare her charm for healing sores and broken bones to ones spoken by charmers such as Janet Brown (1643) and used in the Shetland charm known as the 'Wresting threads':

*The lord rade,*
*And the foal slade;*
*And he righted,*
*Let joint to joint,*
*Bone to bone,*
*And sinew to sinew-*
*Heal in the Holy Ghost's name!*

As you can see it bears similar elements to the charm given by Isobel Gowdie, "*He put the blood to the blood, till all up stood; The lith* (limb) *to the lith* (limb), *Till all, took nith*". Interestingly, charms similar to the 'Wresting Threads' charm is one of the oldest recorded charms in Europe. Other charms of Isobel's, such as her charm "to cure fever," can be compared to W. M. Kerow in Elgin in 1623 (see chapter 1). Some may argue that because of the long periods of time between the recording of Isobel's charms and the others I have given, they cannot be compared. Recent Ethnologists, such as professors Dr. Will Lamb and Neill Martin at the University of Edinburgh have proven through their extensive research that within oral traditions, such as those found in Scotland, folktales, songs, charms, and spells were often carried on through folk memory for many generations without changing.

So, the charms detailed in Isobel's confessions may have been passed onto her by her neighbour or through her very own family members. Also, it was not uncommon for men and women of Isobel's social status to have a second job as a wise woman/man. As Own Davies points out, very few Cunning Folk made a full living off cunning craft, and it would often be a side job to their main occupation. Putting aside the 24 charms dealing with *maleficia,* there were a few which were benevolent such as those for healing sores or broken bones, to cure fever, or for *Bone-Shaw* (sciatica). Isobel's confessions also contained magical practices that were common of the average Charmer. Her other magical charms, which involved ensuring an object be sold, having plentiful fish come to you and the unbewitching of a sick child, were all characteristics of Cunning Folk's repertoire. So, judging by the evidence, she would most likely have been a local wise woman or sorceress.

If Isobel was a wise woman [or whatever term you want to use here], what about her charms involving malefica or diobolica? Although Cunning folk or service magicians did mostly practice beneficial magic that was not to say they did not perform harmful magic, on their enemies or on behalf of their clients. We see it documented countless times that the reputation of the Cunning Folk was both feared and respected by their communities due to their abilities of "laying and talking off diseases," or even luck. We also, only must look through the material of many Grimoires or Black Books to see evidence of curses or harmful magic, let alone some found in Christian prayers and psalms. Just because harmful magic was unlawful did not mean magical practitioners were not performing forms of malefica on others in secret. This also hints at why some Cunning Folk found themselves facing charges of 'using witchcraftis, Sorsarie, and necomancie'. Again, recalling that there were no distinctions made between beneficial magic and witchcraft as in English law. The testimonies regarding diabolica in Isobel Gowdie's confessions reflected that of the "typical" scenes of the Devilish interactions and attendance of the Witches Sabbath as detailed in witch-finding manuals such as the *Malleus Maleficarum* or King James *Demonologie*. Interrogators in the early modern period were deceptive in recording confessions, often writing them in such a way that suggested the accused had said things they had not. Questions such as "did you deny your baptism and consort with the Devil?" turned into statements like "I denied my baptism and gave myself up to the Devil's power".

However, we cannot assume that Isobel's confessions of diabolical actions were entirely influenced by her interrogators. She may have utilised local stories and folklore she would have heard of witches, fairies, and the devil to weave into her diabolical narrative to the interrogators. One thing Emma Wilby speculates is that due to the culture in which Isobel was bought up, as well as being a tradition-bearers of magical charms and antidotes for everyday life, she may have possessed some bardic skills as well. Highland culture is the richest in the bardic arts in Scotland with songs and stories told around the hearthside at night or *cèilidh* houses during the winter months. Given the facts, it's likely Isobel would have developed an artistic flair to her peers as a bardic performer. With that in mind, she would have likely used her skills as a natural storyteller when confessing. It's possible then, that some of her accounts were purely fantasy. However, we cannot make that conclusion based off the fact she had a flair for the theatrics through re-telling local fairy stores heard from her neighbours. As Emma Wilby perfectly puts it:

> When interpreted through the lens of the shamanistic hypothesis, these elements invite us to speculate that when Isobel provided her prosecutors with narratives about feasting and dancing with fairies under the hills and in the cellars of houses, she was not just recounting local fairy lore as some kind of coered fiction, but drawing on memories of shamanistic dreams or trances, consciously undertaken for the benefit of her community, before her arrest.

49

Emma Wilby points out that not all Isobel's shamanic experiences were for the "benefit of her community" as shown by her acts of maleficium, or harmful magic. Wilby coins Isobel's visionary practices as Dark Shamanism' which is compared to the 'ritual predation' practices of the Guyanese *Kanaimà* in which they magically stalk and kill their victims in a "shockingly discriminate way". We know through European witch confessions and folklore that entheogenic agents, or 'Flying Ointments' as they were termed, were used to aid in trance-like states (these ointments may in turn have influenced the witches' sabbath experience). Other causes for visionary experiences like those described in Isobel's testimony may have been unintentional, as recent research points towards a disease known as *Ergot* or 'St Anthony's fire' as it is known by its folk name. Ergot is a fungus that grows on rye and other related plants and produces alkaloids that can cause ergotism in humans and other mammals who consume contaminated grains (*ergot sclerotium*). Ergot alkaloids cause hallucinations, irrational behaviour, convulsions, unconsciousness and even death. Historians sometimes attribute ergot poisoning as the cause for people's visionary experiences during the medieval and early modern periods.

However, the invocation of the Devil's name in Isobel's verbal charms can be explained by a combination of two theories. The first being that this was the Folk Devil, fairy characters viewed by clergy as their Devil or "wee devils. The second theory being that Isobel was calling upon the biblical Devil to aid in harmful magic. In Scotland, unlike some other countries in the British Isles, most of the accounts where accused witches laid claim that their powers or charms were given unto them by the *'gude nichtbouries'*, or fairies than "muckle black deil", or the devil-like their other Celtic neighbours. The 19th-century anthropologist Andrew Lang stated that witches who suffered at Presbyterian hands were merely narrators of fairy stories who trafficked with the dead (or fairies) and from them won medicinal recipes for cures. In Scotland, the fairy-faith has always been a strong backbone in the animistic beliefs of the people, especially in the *gaidhealtachd* or Gaelic-speaking areas of Scotland where they are called the *sìth, sleagh maith* or *daoine beaga*. In fact, during the whole witch-craze, which spread across Scotland, the Gaelic areas to the west had fewer accounts of people being charged with witchcraft. All classes of society during Isobel's time held belief in the fairies, most with great fear but others were concerned with the gifts the fairies could bestow or teach. However, clergymen and the more "educated" peoples of society often referred to the fairies as demons or "wee devils. Rev. Robert Kirk, known for his *The Secret Commonwealth of Elves, Fauns, and Fairies* (1691) deems fairies to be betwixt man and angel, or demons of old. Here you can see where a crossover between the devil and fairies was made during the early modern period in Scotland. In the case of Elizabeth Wright, author Joyce Froome points out that the local authorities referred to the "god" mentioned in Wright's charms as "the devil." Froome concludes that the god of the Cunning Folk was not the same as the one who condemned them, stating that the Christian devil "...was certainly very different from the Lord of the Dance who would lend this divine power for something as trivial as turning cream into butter. Now I am not saying that Cunning Folk were worshiping some ancient god, as expressed in rebuked theories such as Margaret Murray's Witch-Cult Hypothesis but it's true that certain fairy characters during the early modern period (such as hobgoblin Robin Goodfellow) were deemed as the devil and were considered to be the helper spirits of the local wise women/men in rural areas. Perhaps, Isobel Gowdie saw the fairies in the same light when she expressed how she met with the queen and king of Elphame (Fairyland) under the Downie Hills.

In Isobel's confessions both the Devil and the Fairies are mentioned in her magical endeavours, so on the other hand perhaps she would secretly provoke the devil's name in her more harmful spells and charms. In *The Black Books of Elverum*, which is thought to have been written around 1682 (20 years after Isobel's last confession) contains a spell to "stop a drifter" in which the devil is invoked:

*"Oh you Devil before me, return this person who owns this rag or thread, in the Devil's name, in the Devil's name, in the Devil's name."*

Like the accounts given by Isobel Gowdie, wherein God, the Devil, and fairies are utilized in her cunning craft, the Black Books of Elverum holds similar elements in its contents. And, if Isobel were to have owned a Black Book herself, it may have borne some resemblance to those mentioned thus far. Perhaps the Cunning Folk's art lies outside ideals of God and the Devil, Heaven, and Hell!

# THE INFAMOUS BLACK BOOK

The legends and tales of the notorious Black Books have always been quite a popular motif when it comes to folklore associated with witches, wizards, and sorcerers. Throughout Europe these a magic spell book was often handwritten and black leather-bound, as suggested in the title. The name itself use to give people chills up their back. These books were also known as The Book of Cyprianus, *Galdrabók/Galdrakver*, or *Svartkonstbök in the* Scandinavian areas, and as "Black spae-book" in Scotland. Folklore of these infamous Black Books has been displayed in popular occult movies and TV series of today in which Black Books are not just magical manuals but also deemed magical in themselves. For example, in films like Warlock (1989) and Hocus Pocus (1993) the warlock or witch's magical spell book is said to have been written by the devil himself, made from human skin or written in blood, and is powerful that it could not be burnt or damaged in any kind of way. In TV series such as *Sabrina the Teenage Witch* (1996) and *Charmed* (2006), the witch's magic spell book cannot be discarded or touched/read by anyone else other than its owner. Popular connotations of the witch's spell book come from the European folklore of Black Books as well as through the fear of our ancestors regarding witches, sorcerers, and malefica. According to demonological books and witch-hunting manuals, a Black Book was given to a witch or sorcerer by the Devil at the time of her pact or initiation into witchcraft. Once in the possession of the owner, it could not be destroyed or got rid of easily. There are popular stories of people owning such Black Books tearing up, burning, or throwing them into a body of water only to find the book at home, perfectly intact! Other folktales tell of the book being bound in human skin, written in blood, or having black pages with white letters. Some tales say that if someone other than the book's owner opened it, the devil would appear. Some cunning would then be needed to distract the devil until the sorcerer returned home and could deal with the matter. The victim could also simply read the book backwards to dismiss the devil. It was said that if one read the book forwards, the devil would appear. If they read it backwards the devil would leave. However, if one failed to read the book backwards, the devil would gain control of them. Others have it that devilish fiends or spirits would be involved in the opening of the book and would torment the victim. This seems to take influence from the idea of liber spirituum (book of spirits). These books were handwritten by conjurers, containing signs, correspondences, and invocations of demonic and and angelic spirits. These spirits would be invoked through the action of turning to their particular page in the book. Often these Black books were buried with their owner but in some folktales, they would sometimes cause so much grief to the owner that they would take certain measures to rid themselves of the responsibility. One popular idea was that it had to be sold to another less than the price that it was originally bought but if no other person were willing to do so then the local priest could attach an iron chain to it or have it securely enclosed in the church walls. I have heard some folks say that they heard their grandparents tell them about a Black Book having to be bricked up in their local church along with holy relics for fear of the devil or that a witch's curse would be unleashed on the town's folk. The *Book of Hell's Charms* written by Doctor Faust was held in the church at Zellerfeld, Germany secured by an iron chain for some time. Additionally, one method of disposal involved the owner writing his name in the book with his blood before laying it in a secret place within a church together with four shillings clerk's fee. It was said that if a person couldn't dispose of the book before his death, it would go badly for him.

During the last century, some people were unsure whether Black Books circulated amongst the common people or were simply objects of myth and legend. However, there have been a few Black Books recently found around Europe and America is musty old attics, antique chests, or someone's personal library. Some of these book's date from as early as the late 17th century up to the early 20th century. Historian Ottar Evensen says that he knew of one owner of a Black Book who dared not sleep in same room where it was kept. Even in my experience, an old neighbour of mine from Penicuik upon congratulating me on writing the book ended his sentence by saying that the title "gave him the fear". Such published manuscripts which come to mind are *Rún: A magic grimoire*, *Tvaer*

54

*Galdraskraedur. Two Icelandic Books of Magic, The Galdrakver* (all published by the Museum of Icelandic Sorcery & Witchcraft), as well as my favourite, *The Black Books of Elverum.*

Although there are a lot of crossovers when it comes to Black Books and Grimoires, we should not confuse them as being one in the same. All Grimoires are magic books but not all magic books are Grimoires! A Grimoire were often printed manuals for a certain system of ceremonial magic. Black Books, on the other hand, were practical handbooks of local folk magic and medicine for addressing everyday concerns. But to truly understand the difference we must explore deeper into both types of magic books. Grimoires were printed in French or Latin in Europe and were usually a "how-to" guide in conjuring up spirits, demons, and angels by the magician through a system of ceremonial rites, magical seals, and lengthy incantations. The distribution of grimoires was often limited and were very expensive, were usually owned exclusively by people from the higher classes of society. These were people typically concerned with the reputation of "ancient" Eastern magical traditions and their connection to certain biblical characters such as King Solomon, Moses, or St. Cyprian. Another reason why Grimoires caught the attention of "educated" magicians was that they dealt with ritual or ceremonial magic which they classed as a more intellectual and sophisticated kind of magical practice. These purists included finding the elixir of life, searching for hidden treasure or knowledge, conversing with angels, etc. There are some handwritten books of magic, including *The Grimoire of Arthur Gauntlet* and *A Cunning Man's Grimoire*, which, despite their titles, contain a more folk ceremonial type of magic. Although these two manuscripts are ritualistic in context, they are not copies of any typical Grimoire. Instead, these books contained selected tested experiments or content suiting the sorcerer's magical practice.

Black books have much of a reputation in the history of magic than grimoires, until in recent centuries the act of writing itself was imbued with occult and hidden power, a belief originating from the mysterious medieval scribes. So powerful was the written word that during the Middle Ages people feared a scribe's "book curse", written in the first few pages of a book warning all those who stole or intentionally damaged it would be punished by the wrath of God. Magical charms and verses for healing or against harm, often biblical in context, were deemed most effective when they were handwritten on scraps of paper or parchment and worn on the body. We see examples of this right up to the 20th century and this practice is still performed today. Black Books, putting aside the folklore about being written by the devil, seemed to have greater magical reputations based on that of the magicians or cunning folk who wrote them. As Owen Davies states in *Grimoire: A History of Magic Books* (2009):

> "Magicians had no personal influence over the creation of print grimoires, could not imbue them with magical power through the ritual use of materials. The printed book was not integral to magic, rather a record of it. Magicians were merely purchasers of a product."

To the mind of a magician or layman, print drained the power from magic books that they once had. The action of the pen to paper lay at the hands of folk magic and print at literacy magic. In some modern magical traditions, practitioners keep a handwritten notebook or journal containing spells, charms, and magical operations. One such example is the Book of Shadows within Wiccan traditions. In fact, The Book of the Shadows written by Gerald Brosseau Gardner is a combination of high (ceremonial) and low (operational) magic. Today, grimoires can also refer to one's personal spell book.

One thing to keep in mind is that the term Black Book was used generically to describe many different manuals, much like the term Good Book is used to describe the bible. In Scandinavia, as mentioned before, a *book of Cyprianus* was referred to as a Black Book. In Scotland, the legendary *Red Book of Appin* (which contained marvellous charms for the curing or diseases and cattle as well as promoting fertility in herds) was said to have been obtained from the Devil through great trickery. According to one folktale, a man obtained a Black Book after riding a horse to a meeting of Witches. He was able to get a hold of the book and ride off despite being chased by the devil and all his servants. The manuscript in the 'A

Cunning man's Grimoire' is referred to as the "Secret of Secrets". This has no relation to the Grimoire *Secretum Secretorum*, instead it was simply what was inscribed in the books as its title.

While the Black Book tradition was most popular in areas of Northern Europe, it was also present in Scotland. A woman from the Parish of Ematris (Ireland), Mrs. M. A. McAdoo reported in 1930 that Black Books were bought in Scotland by Irish workers who went over during harvest time. However, it was against the law at the time to buy or sell such books. To seek out a Black Book, a person had to place £1 in certain place. McAdoo went on to say that "while one watched a hand appeared, took the money and shortly afterward put the required book in it its place." McAdoo also said that at the beginning of many Black Books the following words would be written:

> *Read me through*
> *But pursue me not,*
> *For if you do*
> *Hell and damnation will be your lot.*

Mr. G. M. Nelson of Gott (Shetland) recalled how a similar phrase was written in a Black Book. Nelson remembered an old man who assured him that he had seen such a book on whose prefatory pages appeared the words, "Cursed is he that persueth me."

The most famous magician to have had a Black Book in their possession was the 13th-century wizard of North (Balwearie) Sir Michael Scott. Dempster says that he remembers hearing in his youth that Michael Scott's magic books were real but that they could not be opened for fear that spirits would be invoked. Michael Scott's Black Book is mentioned in John Layden's ballad 'Lord Soulis' (1802-3), Walter *Scott's The Lay of the Last Minstrel* (1805), and in John Hogg's novel *The Three Perils of man* (1822). In the latter, Scott's magic book is referred to as The Book of Might or as a "black spae-book. In Layden's story, the Wizard Lord Soulis is buried with Michael Scott's book which is later taken from the grave by True Thomas, the laird of Ersyltoun:

> *The black spae-book from his breast he took,*

57

*Impress'd with many a warlock spell:*
*And the book was wrote by Michael Scott,*
*Who held in awe the fiends of hell.*

Others who were said to have possessed Black Books were millers. In Scotland, and other countries, millers have a long reputation of being "men or skill" or possessing occult powers akin to witches and charmers. There is a story about a Black Book belonging to a miller near Horsens (Denmark). One day a journeyman slipped into the miller's private room and, out of curiosity, read out loud from the book. Satan himself then appeared before the journeyman and asked his commands. The miller took the book from the journeyman and, reading it, tried to have the fiend depart. But the miller could not drive Satan away without giving him a task. So, the miller took a sieve and commanded him to bale water with it from the millpond. Because Satan was unable to do so he was obligated to take his departure through the air, leaving behind him a most loathsome stench.

In Scottish legends regarding Black Books, like in northern European folklore, it was said they not only contained several magical spells and formulas but possessed magical powers themselves.

Penny Fielding, in her article "Black Books: Sedition, Circulation, and the Lay of the Last Minstrel," states that in Scottish romantic literature, Black Books were given "double status" as being both a magical object and a textbook of magic. Fielding points out that this was because the "Scot's language, where 'glamour,' a magical spell, is cognate with 'grammar,' or book-learning.

The lowlanders did not shy away from the Black Arts and books dealing with it. This was especially to brigands such as the moss-troopers, who Bishop Nicholson said that *"our borderers are not, at this day, utter strangers to the black art of their ancestors. I met with a gentleman on the neighbourhood who shows me a book of spells and magical receipts, taken two or three days before in the pocket of one of our moss-troppers."* It seems that Orkney and Shetland were the most renowned in Scotland for the distribution of Black Books, as Ernest W. Marwick wrote:

The Book of the Black Art, a Handbook of magic, was known by reputation throughout Orkney. The few who had seen it declared that it was printed in white characters on black paper. It not only contained all kinds of spells and charms, but it conferred on its owner the power to put them into effective operation. There was one grave drawback to owning it. If anyone died with it in his possession, he and the book were claimed immediately by the book's author, the Devil. One could only get rid of it by selling it for a smaller coin than one had given for it, or by persuading someone to accept it as a gift. A man in Sandwick (O) took the book far out to sea, then threw it overboard in a sack weighted with stones. When he got home, the book lay in its usual place on the kitchen table. A girl in Dandy (O) who had unsuspectingly accepted a copy from Recchel T------, a local witch, tried desperately to destroy the book. Once she flung it over Grunavi Head, but it was back in her bedroom before she got home. In both instances, the terrified possessors of the Book of the Black Art were relieved of the volume by a clergyman. The Rev. Charles Clouston (died 1884) bought the Sandwick copy and buried it in the manse garden. The Sanday copy was accepted by the Rev. Matthew Armour (died 1903).

There were a few other regions of Scotland where Black Books were mentioned to have been used by charmers and Wise Men/Women. The Scottish folk healer Bartie Patersoune, who was executed for the crime of witchcraft and sorcery in 1607, had a Black Book containing the SATOR ROTAS square, magical symbols, and other occult diagrams. The documents confiscated from Bartie Paterson in 1607 contained a mix of Latin and English and included occult tables, signs, and symbols, presumably derived from either a book or one of the various magical manuscripts circulating at the time. Bessie Wright, who was brought before the Perth presbytery and subsequently a secular court in 1628, also claimed literature as her source of power. Her skill derived from a book that had belonged to her father and grandfather, and which was, she said, a thousand years old. It is telling, however, that she was illiterate and had to rely on her son to read out the relevant sections to her. Alexander Drummond confessed to having a book of cures, which may simply have been a book of herbal charms rather than a grimoire. Thomas Muir (1793), at his trial, confessed that he possessed "the most demonic book of all" which many people would have thought of as a Black Book during the early modern period.

Black Books themselves were also used as form of talisman since they were reputed to have been imbued with magical powers by either the writer or the Devil. Here are some ways which Black Books were used:

*For protection whilst traveling or against evil spirits, carry the book in your left coat pocket.*

*To have someone sleep like the dead, place this book under their bed before midnight.*

*To invoke the presence of the Devil, open the book and recite the Lord's Prayer backwards.*

*To make a pact with the devil, sign the Black Book in your own blood.*

*To rid yourself of witchcraft or the Devil, sell the book to someone who is willing less than the price that you bought it, or have the priest bless it on a Sunday.*

*To seal a deal or contract with someone, shake hands over the book. To make an unbroken oath place you left on the book and pronounce the oath or promise.*

# THE BLACK BOOK OF
# ISOBEL GOWDIE

*"For Isobel Gowdie"* by Johnny Decker Miller

*"I denyed my baptisme, and did put the one*

*of my hands to the crown of my head,*

*and the other to the sole of my foot, and then*

*renounced all betwixt my two hands over to the
Devil. He was in the Reader's desk, and a black book*

*in his hand."*

As previously mentioned, it is uncertain whether Isobel Gowdie or others accused held such a Black Book in their possession. There is one reference in Gowdie's confession of the Devil holding a "black book in his hand" during the renouncement of her Christian faith. The presence of Black Books during the making of pacts with the Devil was a popular in European belief. It was most likely Isobel would have been illiterate as many people were during the early modern period. So, I have complied to together a Black Book from the magical content that she relayed in her confessions.

I have kept to the authenticity of the content submitted in the trial, except for modifying the wording to modern English or reconstructed verses where words are otherwise unrecognizable or damaged in the original manuscript. For example, Isobel's charm 'To have an object sold' had a few words/sentences which were damaged but since it seemed to resemble the famous toothache charm, I was able to reconstruct the charm like so:

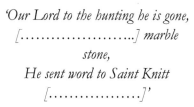

| | |
|---|---|
| *'Our Lord to the hunting he is gone,* | " Peter sat on a marble stone |
| *[......................] marble* | weeping, |
| *stone,* | Christ came past and said, ' |
| *He sent word to Saint Knitt* | What aileth thee, Peter? ' |
| *[.................]'* | ' O my Lord, my God, my |
| | tooth doth ache! ' |
| | ' Arise, O Peter, go thy way, |
| | thy tooth shall ache no more! |

The reconstruction for this charm can be seen further on in this book. I have also added in some areas within this Black Book other content relating to Isobel's magical repertoire such as Robert Grave's "Fith-fath" poem or the charm 'To protect someone against storm at sea' mentioned in the *Highland Chapbook*.

I am aware that some people might feel a bit uncomfortable at the idea of making invocations in the Devil's name but do not stress. I implore readers that there is no harm in modifying Isobel's spells and charms to fit with your practice, including substituting names of different spirits, saints, or deities. As I always say to modern practitioners who are conflicted, for folk magic to continue to survive it must change with the times.

**When I became a witch....** *I was going betwixt the towns of Drumdewin and the Headis: I met with the devil and there covenanted in a manner with him, and I promised to meet him in the night time in the Kirk of Auldearne and this I did, and the thing I did there that night I denied my baptism, and did put one of my hands to the crown of my head and the other to the sole of my foot, and then renounced all betwixt my two hands over to the Devil, he was in the readers desk and a **black book** in his hand: Margret Brodie in Auldreane held me up to the Devil to be baptised by him, and he marked me on the shoulder, and sucked out my blood at the mark and spat it in his hand, and sprinkling it on my head said I baptise thee, "Janet in my own name", and within a while we all removed ourselves from the devils presence.*

*I was then given onto me my familiar spirit, 'the seventh spirit is called the Red Reiver and he's my personal spirit. he waits upon me and is always dressed in black.*

# To raise the winds or Rain

*Whenever we raised the wind, we take a rag of cloth and wet it in water and we take a beetle (washing board) and knock the rag on a stone, and we say thrice over:*

**I knock this rag upon this stane,**

**To raise the wind (or rain), in the Devil's name;**

**It shall not lie until I please again!**

*When we would lay the wind, we dry the rag, and say thrice over:*

**We lay the wind in the Devil's name,**

**It shall not rise while we [or I] like to raise it again!**

*And if the wind will not lie instantly after we say this, we call upon our Spirits, and say to him:*

**Thief! Thief! I conjure the wind and cause it to lie.**

*We have no power of rain, but we will raise the wind as we please....*

There is an old Orkney charm for making it rain wherein a witch goes to a stream or pool and throws up water in the devil's name. Although Isobel said in her confessions that she had power no over the rain, I have used this charm to bring rain too and it has worked just as well! Raising storms or bringing rain was a common element which the witch or sorcerer held a skill in. It was a popular trade amongst cunning folk to "sell winds" to sailors and fishermen. Wise Men and Women would sell a three-knotted rag or cord and it was through the untying of the knots that favourable winds, needed to set the sails of a ship, would be produced. In fact, Bessie Miller of

Stromness was said, at the age of a hundred, to be famous for selling favourable winds to sailors for the moderate price of a sixpence. A woodcut depicting sorcerers both selling the winds and brewing up a storm, resembling the very actions described by Isobel, appears in the *Olaus Magnus Historia de gentibus septentrionalibus* (1555) as pictured above.

## To Protect someone from storm at sea

This spell, from the *Highland Chapbook*, to protect someone at sea is reminiscent of Isobel's style of magic and has similar elements to her wind raising charm. A wax image is made in the likeness of the person you wish to be protected at sea. Water is then dashed all around' it whilst chanting softly:

*I hold thee safe in the devil's name*

*Unscathed of water shalt thou remain.*

*Unhurt of wind, undrowned in sea*

*Safe so long as pleaseth me.*

*I lay this wind in the devil's name*

*I shall not raise till I please again*

*May the winds lie hushed amd still*

*And raise no more without I will.*

## A charm for spirit flight or to spirited off to Elfhame

67

*When I wish to take flight or be fae away, I take wild straw or bean stalks and put them betwixt our feet and day thrice:*

*Horse and*

*Hattock, in the Devil's name!*

*Or we would say thrice:*

*Horse and Hattock, horse and go,*

*Horse and pellatris, ho! ho!*

*And then we would fly away where we would be, even as would fly upon a highway, we will fly like straws when we please. Wild straws and corn straws will be like horses to us when we put*

*them betwixt our feet, and anyone who sees these straws in a whirlwind, and do not sanctify themselves, we will shoot them dead at our pleasure. Anyone that are shot be us, their souls will go to heaven, but their bodies remain with us, and will fly away as horses to us all, small as straws.*

Sarah Anne Lawless, writer of the online website/blog *The Witch of Forest Grove*, did some extensive research into this specific charm of Isobel's and discovered that the words "Horse and Hattock" were popular within fairy lore. It was said that fairies used these words when they wished to move from place to place. This fact is mentioned in Scottish Folktales, such as *Fairy transportation* published by Sir George Douglas, *The Doom Well of St. Madron* by Rev. R.S Hawer, and *The Black Dwarf* by Sir Walter Scott. Sarah Anne Lawless explains that the Scots word 'Hattock' is the fairy sign for mounting and riding off.

Additionally, the word "pallatris" comes from the French "paillet" meaning a bundle of straw. Both explanations seem fitting given Isobel's testimony of the magic rite she performed.

Also, schoolboys near Forres during the mid-17th century would playfully say the fairy phrase 'horse and hattock with my top!' to conjure a whirlwind to lift their toy spinning tops.

Here is a similar charm recorded by a man dwelling in Houll, Mid Yell (Shetland) which was said to be spoken by the trows (fairies) whenever they were "oot an' aboot":

| | |
|---|---|
| *Up hors, up hedick,* | *Up horse, up Heddick,* |
| *Up will ridn bolwind* | *Up will I ride a whirlwind,* |
| *An I kin I's reyd among yu* | *And I know I'll ride among you!* |

## To go into a Hare, Cat or Crow

*When we go in the shape of a hare, we say thrice over:*

I shall go into a hare,

With sorrow, and such, and mickle

care;

And I shall go in the Devil's name,

Aye, until I come hame again!

*The likeness of a cat*

**69**

*I shall go into a cat,*

*With sorrow, and such, and a black shot!*

*And I shall go in the Devil's name,*

*Aye, until I come Hame again!*


*The likeness of a crow*

*I shall go into a crow,*

*With sorrow, and such, and a black thraw!*

*And I shall go in the Devil's name,*

*Aye, until I come hame again!*


*And to return to your proper shape:*

*Hare! hare! [cat or crow] God send thee care!*

*I am in a hare's likeness just now,*

*But I shall be in a woman's (or man's) likeness even now.*


## 𝕿o turn another into animal shape:

*If we go in the shape of a cat, a crow, a hare, or any other likeness, etc., to any of our neighbour's houses, we will say:*

**70**

*I (or we) conjure thee go with us (me)!*

*Or*

*Devil speed thee, go thow with me!*

*And immediately they will turn into the shape of a cat etc…and go with us.*

Isobel confessed that she *"cannot turn into the likeness of a lamb or a dove"*. Perhaps this a reference to the Holy Spirit being represented by a dove and Christ being the "Lamb of God." Because of the diabolical nature of Isobel's practice of Witchcraft, she would not be able to assume such holy forms. Although no human can actually change their shape, perhaps this action was more of a psychoactive and spiritual action than a physical one. Much like the Scandinavian concept of *fylgja*, or fetch spirit, whose form the conjurer assumes through the use of hallucinogenic plants. This magical practice was not uncommon within Scotland, especially within Gaelic speaking areas where *fìth-fàth* or *fàth-fìth* was a Gàidhlig term for either rendering oneself invisible by a magical mist or the action of shapeshifting into animal form.

Kalden Mercury has done a beautiful rendition of Isobel's shape-shifting charm on his YouTube channel titled: *In the Devil's Name* (2021).

## 𝔄 shape shifting or *fìth-fàth* song

This poem is a modern adaption of Isobel Gowdie's shapeshifting charm, written by the poet Robert Graves in his book *The White Goddess* (1948). The poem follows thus: -

*'O I shall go into a hare, with sorrow and sighing and mickle care. And I shall go in the Devil's name, Aye, 'til I be fetched hame. Hare take heed of*

*a bitch greyhound, for here come I in Our Lady's name, All to fetch thee hame.'*

*'Cunning and art he did not lack, but aye her whistle would fetch him back.'*

*'Yet I shall go into a trout, with sorrow and sighing and mickle doubt, And show thee many a merry game, Ere that I be fetched hame. Trout take heed of an otter lank, will harry thee close from bank to bank, For here come I in our Lady's name, All to fetch thee hame.'*

*'Cunning and art he did not lack, but aye her whistle would fetch him back.' '*

*Yet I shall go into a bee, with mickle dread and horror of thee, And flit to hive in the Devil's name, Ere that I be fetched hame again. Bee, take heed of a swallow hen, will harry thee close, both butt and ben, For here I come in Our Lady's name, All but I fetch thee hame.'*

*'Cunning and art he did not lack, but aye her whistle would fetch him back.' 'Yet I shall go into a mouse, and haste me to the miller's house, there in his corn to have good game, Ere that I be fetched hame. Mouse, take heed of a white tib-cat, that never was baulked of mouse or rat, For I'll crack thee bones in Our Lady's name, thus shalt thou be fetched hame.'*

*'Cunning and art he did not lack, but aye her whistle would fetch him back.'*

Certain verses in this poem/song hold magical indications, as Graham King points out that 'fetching back' and 'fetching home' refers to 'changing back into human form'. Folk musicians such as

Pixi Morgan and Damh the Bard do beautiful renditions of the poem in song entitled: *'fith fath'* song.

## To have a broom or stool appear as the likeness of yourself.

*Lest our husbands should miss me out of my bed, I put in a besom, or a three-legged stool, beside them, and say thrice over:*

*I lay down this besom (or stool) in the [Devil's] name,*

*Let it (him/her) not stir till I come home again!*

*And immediately it seems a woman, by the side of my husband, we cannot turn in the likeness of a besom or stool.*

In the Scottish folktale The Witches of Delnabo (George Douglas 1901) a farmers' wives would leave brooms by their husband's side during the night. They did this to sneak off at night to gather with other witches at a magical pool beside a hill known as "Craic-pol-nain" or the Craig of the Birdspool. In the morning, the husbands would be unaware of their wives' absence.

## To have commodities sold

*When my husband wanted his beef sold, I use to put a shallow's feather at the head of the beast and say thrice over:*

*I put out this [beef] in the Devil's name,*

*That mickle silver and good price come hame!*

*whenever I wanted any other commodities to sell well, such as a horse, cattle, or cloth she would say thrice:*

*Our Lord to hunting, he is gone;*

*Standing on a marble stone,*

*He sent word to Saint Knitt for gifts bestrewn!*

This charm had passages which were unclear or marked, so I have reconstructed this charm by comparing it with similar charms. This particular charm seems to bear similarity to another charm for toothache involving St. Peter. In Isobel's charm, St. Knitt refers to St. Nick or Nicholas who is the patron saint of gift-giving. Here he is called upon to aid the reciter in selling their objects. Often, when I am using this charm, I will say both the charms to sell an object and finish off by saying: "*By heaven or by hell, this [item] will sell!!*".

## To have plenty of fish come to you.

*And when we took the fruit of the fish from the fishermen, we went to the shore, before the boat came in, and on the shoreside we would say three times:*

*The fishers are gone to the sea,*

74

*And they will bring home fish to me;*

*They will bring them home until the boat,*

*But they shall get of them but the smaller sort*

So we either steal a fish, or buy a fish, or get a fish from them for nothing, one or more. And with that we have the fruit of the entire catch in the boat, and the fish the fishermen are left with are just froth, etc.

When Isobel speaks of the *"fruit of the fish"* she could be meaning the *Toradh* or substance from the fishes at sea.

## The devils Grace

*We eat this meat in the devillis name,*

*With sorrow and sych and meikle*

*shame:*

*We sall destroy hows and hald:*

*Both sheep and noat intill the fald.*

*Little good sall come to the fore*

*Of all rest of the little store.*

## To heal any sores or broken limbs

*When we want to heal any wound or broken limb, we say three times:*

*He put the blood to the blood, till all up stood;*

*The lith to the lith, Till all took nith;*

*Our Lady charmed her dearly Son, With her tooth and her*

*tongue, And her ten fingers,*

*In the name of the Father, the Son, and the Holy Ghost!*

Although no action was given in Isobel's confession alongside this charm, it was common in folk medicine to perform the "laying of the hands. Additionally, a smooth piece of stone would at times be rubbed gently over the afflicted area whilst saying a charm.

## To cure Bone-Shaw (sciatica) or pain in the haunch

*For bone-shaw or pain in the haunch, I would say over the person:*

*We are here three Maidens charming for the bean-shaw;*

*the man of the Midle-earth, blew beaver, land-fever, maneris of stooris,*

*the Lord fleigged (terrified) the Fiend with his holy candles and yard foot-stone!*

*There she sits, and here she is gone!*

*Let her never come here again!*

## To cure a fever

*For fevers, I would say over the person:*

*I forbid the quaking-fevers, the sea-*

*fevers, the land-fevers, and all the fevers that God*

*ordained,*

*out of the head, out of the heart, out of the*

*back, out of the sides, out of the knees, out of the*

*thighs, from the points of the fingers to the nibs of*

*the toes;*

*net fall the fevers go, some to the hill,*

*some to the heep, some to the stone,*

*some to the stock.*

*In St. Peter's name, St. Paul's name, and all*

*the Saints of Heaven.*

*In the name of the Father, the Son, and of the Holy Ghost!*

Isobel's charm was not unlike that employed by W. M Kerow in Elgin in 1623, which was as follows:

*The quaquand fewer and the trembling fewer*

*And the sea fewer and the land fewer,*

*Bot and the head fewer and the hart fewer,*

*And all the feweris that God creatit.*

**77**

*In sanct Johnes name, Sanct Peteris name,*

*And all the Sancts of heavin's name*

*Our Lord Jesus Chrystis Name*

## To heal a child who is bewitched.

*Isobel said that if a child be forespoken or bewitched, she would take the cradle .... through it thrice, and then a dog through it; and then shake the belt above the fire and then cast it down on the ground, till a dog or cat go over it, that the sickness may come upon the dog or cat. The Cunning man of Tarbruith Andro [Andrew] Man (1598) did a similar magical action in curing illness where he put a man nine times forwards through a piece of yarn and transferred the sickness to a cat, which he put backwards through the same piece of yarn.*

## To cause illness by elf-arrow

*As for elf arrowheads, the Devil shapes them with his own hand, and then delivers them to Elf-boys, who shape and trim them with a sharp thing like a packing needle. When I was in Elfland I saw them shaping and making them. Those that make them are little folk, hollow [barrel-chested?] and hunchbacked. They speak gruffly, like. When the Devil gives the bolts to us, we say*

*I shoot you man in the Devil's name,*

*He shall not go healed hame!*

*And this shall be always true;*

*There shall not be one bit of him alive.*

These elf-arrows were often just Neolithic arrowheads used in cursing. Although quite hard to find now in Britain, replica arrowheads made of flint or gemstone can often be found in your local Esoteric shops.

## A charm baggie to cause death.

*On the first Monday of the month, take a bag made of hare's liver, the fleshly guts & galls of a toad, the nail pairings of the fingers and toes [of the victim], and swing it in the direction of the person. Bessie Wilson, a member of our Coven did this on Thomas Reid and he died.*

## To make or keep a person sick.

*In the winter 1660 when Harry Forbes, minister at Auldearne was sick; we made a bag chopped the flesh and guts of a toad, ears of barley, bits of clouts (rags) and the liver of a hare, along with Mr Forbes's nail clips from his feet and hands. We steeped this all night amongst water and say thrice: --*

*He is lying in his bed; he is laying sick and sore;*

*Let him lie onto his bed two months and three days more!*

*Let him lie onto his bed; let him lie into it sick and sore;*

*Let him lie onto his bed months two and*

*three days more!*

*He shall lie onto his bed; he shall lie in it sick and sore;*

*He shall lie onto his bed two months and three days more!*

For those modern folk magic practitioners who wish to use this charm, I would firstly recommend you think long and hard before doing so. Additionally, use alternative ingredients for a toad or hare as it is not only cruel, but they are both becoming extinct today. I have substituted the ingredients for pieces of meat from a Sunday roast dinner with a few pinches of barley along with the person's personal effects and/or their name on a piece of paper. I put them in a cloth bag or pouch and that place that beside a fast-flowing river, tying it to a nearby tree or branch with string, allowing it to steep in the running water.

Isobel further said that after having the bag steep in water for some time she would swing it, perhaps in a *widdershins* or *tauthsil* (anti-clockwise) direction, whilst chanting the charm again thrice more.

Another way this charm can be adapted and used, which I have done myself, is to aid or keep someone asleep. If someone is suffering from restless sleep, place some barley, along with their personal effects/name and some graveyard dirt into a bag. Then, holding the bag by its string or cord, swing it up and down over the bed whilst saying thrice:

*He/she shall lie onto his bed; he/she shall lie in it snug and snore.*

*He shall lie onto his bed two hours, and three minutes more!*

This chant is only an example and can be tailored to how many hours you wish the patient to sleep for. The charm can be tied to a bedpost or placed under the pillow or bed itself.

# To harm using a clay dollie

Four years ago me and my husband along with Isobel Gowdie and Bessie and Margaret Wilson from Aulderne made a clay image of the Laird 'o Park's eldest son. My husband brought the clay home in a corner of his plaid.

 It was made in my house with the Devil himself present. We broke the clay up into meal-sized pieces and sifted it in a sieve and mixed it with water I brought home from the Rood Well in an earthenware jar, repeating the words the Devil had taught us, saying them in his name as we mixed it. Then we were all on our knees with our hair about our faces and our hands raised to the Devil, staring at him as we repeated the words three times:

*In the Devils name,*

*we power in this water among this meal,*

*For lang duyning and ill heal;*

*We put it into the fire,*

*That it may be burnt*

*both stik and stowre.*

*It falbe brunt, with owr will.*

*As any sickle upon a kill.*

We put its face near the fire until it shrivelled with the heat, then we put it amongst the hot embers until it glowed red like a coal. After that we would roast it now and then; every other day a part of it would be well roasted. All the Laird's male children will suffer by it if it isn't found and broken, as well as those who've been born and died already. It was still being put in and out of the fire in the Devil's name. It was hung up on a peg. It's still there in John Taylor's house, and has a clay cradle around it.

# To take the Fruit away of any person's midden or dunghill

WE putt this until this hame,

In our Lord the Devils name.

The first hands that handles thee,

Brunt and scalded fall they be!

We sall destroy hows and bald,

With the sheip and nout until the sold,

And little sal come to the fore

Of all the reft of the little-store


## To take the fruit away from a field

When we took away the fruit of his corn and all, and we shared it amongst two of our covens. When we steal corn at Lammas we take only about two sheaves when the corn is ripe, or two stalks of kale, or thereabouts and that gives us the fruit of the cornfield or kaleyard where they grew. We did this and say thrice:

We cut this come in our Lord the Devils name,

And we shall haw the fruit of it hame!

On many occasions I have used this spoken charm when harvesting corn to make corn dollies at Lammas or even when harvesting certain plants or tree branches for magical purposes

# SPELLS & CHARMS OF THE ACCUSED

*Let warlocks grim an' wither'd hags*
*Tell how wi' you on ragweed nags*
*They skim the muirs an' dizzy crags*
*Wi' wicked speed;*
*And in kirk-yards renew their leagues,*
*Owre howket dead.*

Rorbet Burns. *Address to the Deil* (1785)

Much like Isobel Gowdie, quite a number of charmers and Wise men/women were convicted under the Scottish Witchcraft. The number of charmers convicted were greater than those in England. Owen Davies, in his article titled '*A Comparative Perspective on Scottish Cunning-folk and Charmers*', explains that the reason for this was that:

> The Scottish Statute makes no distinctions at all. Witchcraft and beneficial magic were treated as one undifferentiated capital crime, which certainly accurately reflected Calvinist theological thinking.

Although the 1563 Scottish Statutes against 'using witchcraftis, sorsarie and necromancie' appeared in the same year as England's more detailed laws 'against conjurations, enchantments, and witchcraft', it was not inspired by the English but more directly from Calvinist thinking. The Scottish Statutes were briefer than the English one. This meant that anyone practicing any form of magic, even those who consulted magical specialists, would be convicted, and possibly sentenced to death. In England, as well as other countries people who were found guilty of charming or cunning-craft were hardly ever punished to the same degree as witchcraft. Instead, those found guilty were often given penalties such as fines, branding, penance, time in the pillory, imprisonment, or banishment, then death.

Other famous accused cunning-folk and charmers were Dr. John Fian and Agnes Sampson, both of whom had a reputation for their magical activities long before they were prosecuted during the North Berwick trials of 1590. Bessie Dunlop, the wise woman of Lynn, cured people by using herbs and advice given to her by her ghostly companion Thomas Reid. Dunlop was prosecuted for witchcraft in 1579. To mention a few, but the most interesting account of a magical practitioner being convicted under the Scottish Witch Act was the case of Alexander Drummond. He was a charmer of Auchterarder and seemed to have a lot of local support for charges of witchcraft against him to be dropped, much so that Alexander had to be transported from Stirling Tolbooth to Tolbooths in Linlithgow and Edinburgh until he was eventually put to executed in 1629. Some 20 years after his death, a campaign was launched to posthumously clear his name with letters written to the King in October and December 1646.

We know so much more about the practices of magical specialists in Scotland than anywhere else in Britain is because Scottish wise men/women and charmers were equally, if not more, prone to secular prosecution and execution. Folk magic was often carried on by oral tradition and very little information about the activities of magical practitioners was written down(?). However, these practices have been preserved by early folklorists. Thanks to the work of *The Survey of Scottish Witchcraft* at the University of Edinburgh, you can now search through their database of over 4,000 cases of witch trials in Scotland.

I will also add that it is important for the modern practitioner to have a record of where these spells and charms come from and who recited them before. This is because we are taking part in the red thread or heritage of these magical workings when we use them. Before I begin to use a charm or spell, I like to give my respect and call on the aid of those who used them before me. You may want to say a prayer or light a candle to the ancestor of that charm or spell, for example, I would say something like this:

> *Agnes Sampson, the wise woman of Keith,*
> *Famed witch of North Berwick,*
> *phantom spirit of Holyrood Palace.*
> *I work this charm as you did work it,*
> *I speak them as you did speak them,*
> *Words of your words, hands of your hands,*
> *Breath of your breath, I beseech thee,*
> *As I work the charms of your Black and White prayers.*

Then I would cross myself in the name of the holy trinity and the spirits of earth, sea, and sky, and then I begin to perform the desired charm or spell.

## Agnes Sampson's Black and White prayers

### (28th January 1591)

### The White Prayer
*I trow in almycte God that wrocht*
*Baith heavin and erth and all of nocht;*
*In to his deare Son Chryste Jesus,*
*In to that myghtie Lord I trow,*

*Wes gottin of the Holy Gaist,*
*Borne of the Virgin marie;*
*Steppit to heaven that all weil than,*
*And sittis att his faderis rycht hand.*
*He baid us cum, and therto dome,*
*Bayth quick and deid, as he thocht quhome*
*I trow als in the Holy Gaist;*
*In haly kirk, my hip is maist,*
*That holy schip quhair hallowaris winnis,*
*To ask forgevenes of my sinnis,*
*And syne to ryis in flesh and bane,*
*The lyffe that nevir mair hes gane,*
*Trow sayis, Lord lovit mot ye be,*
*That formd and maid man kynd of me,*
*Thou coft me on the aly crose,*
*And hent me body, saull, and voce,*
*And ordanit meto heavenis blis;*
*Quhairfoir, I think ye, Lord of this;*
*To pray the thame, to pray to me;*
*And keip me fra that fellown dae;*
*And frome the syne that saull wald slay,*
*Thou, Lord for thy bytter passioun,*
*To keip me from syn and warldie schame,*
*And endless damnatioun.*
*Grant me the ioy newir gane,*
*Sweit Jesus Chrisus. Amen*

### The Black Prayer

*All kindes of illis that weir may be,*
*In Chrystis name I coniure ye,*
*I coniure ye baith mair and les*
*Will all the vertewis of the mes:*
*And rycht sa be the naillis sa'*
*That naillit Jesus and na ma;*
*And rycht sa be the samin blude,*
*That raikit owir the ruithfull rude;*
*Furth of the flesch and of the bane,*

*And in the urd and in the stane.*
*I coniure ye in Godis name!*

**Translation:**

## White prayer

I trust in almighty God that is right.
Both heaven and earth and everyone from night
In his dear son, Christ Jesus
And to all almighty Lord I trust,
Was gotten of the Holy ghost,
Born of the Virgin Mary,
Stepped into heaven that's all good,
And sat at his father's right hand.

He bid us to come, and therefore done,
Both quick and dead, as he thought when
I pray also in the [name of] holy ghost;
In holy church, my hope is most,
That holy ship where hollowed wins,
To ask forgiveness of my sins,
And syne to raise in flesh and bone,
The left that never more his gone,
Pray says, Lord's love let it be,
That formed and made mankind of me.
Thou nailed me on the holy cross,
And bent my body, soul, and voice,
And ordered me to heavens bliss;
Therefore, I thank you, Lord of this;
And all your hollowed love be,
To pray to them, to pray to me;
And keep me from that fellow fae (fairy);
And from the sin that the soul would slay,
Thou, Lord for my bitter passion,
To keep me from sin and worldly shame,

And endless Damnation.
Grant me the joy, never will it be gone,
Sweet Jesus Christ. Amen

### The Black Prayer

All kinds of ill that ever may be,
In Christ's name I conjure ye,
With all the virtues of the mass:
And right so be the nails so,
That nailed Jesus and the more:
And right so be the same blood,
That scrounge over the raftful rod,
Formed of the flesh and of the bone,
And in the urn and in the stone.
I conjure ye in God's Name.

---

Thomas Davidson. *Rowan tree and Red Thread*

## Isobel Strachan's charm to stop a wife-beater.

### (1597)

When the wife of Walter Ronaldson consulted Isobel about her husband's habit of beating her, she took several pieces of paper, sewed them together with different coloured threads, and buried them in the barn among some corn. From then on Walter did never strike his wife or found fault with her.

---

Pitcairn, Robert. *Ancient Criminal Trials in Scotland*

# Janet Brown's Bone-Setting Spell

## (1643)

*Our lord forth raide'*

*His foal foot slade;*

*Our Lord down Lighted'*

*Saying, 'flesh to flesh, blood to blood, and*

*Bone to bone'.*

---

George F. Black. *Witchcraft in Scotland*

# Mary Sproat's Bone-Setting Spell

## (1821)

*Esus rade ane he slade,*

*First be lichtit,*

*Syne be lichtit,*

*Knuckle tae knuckle,*

*Bone tae Bone,*

*Join ie Haly Ghoste's Name*

### Translation:

Jesus' rode and he slated,

First be lighted,

After be lighted,

Knuckle to Knuckle,

Bone to Bone,

Join all in the Holy Ghost's name.

---

Michael Howard. *Scottish Witches and Warlocks*

## 𝕭artie 𝕻aterson's 𝖘pell for curing ills

### (Dec. 18, 1607)

*I charge thee for arrowschot,*
*For doorschot, for wombschot,*
*For liverschot, for lungschot,*
*For hertschot- all the maist:*
*In the name of the father, the sone, and the Haly Ghaist*
*Amen!*

## 𝕻aterson's charm for lifting water.

A man named Alexander Crichton came to Bartie to be cured of his illness. She prescribed a draught of Loch water to him which he was to lift it and say nine times before drinking:

*I lift this watter in the name*
*of the father, the Sone, and Haly Gaist,*
*To do guid for thair health for whom it is liftit*

---

Thomas Davidson. *Rowan tree and Red Thread*

## 𝕸argaret 𝕸ac𝕶irdy's 𝖘pell

## for "for ane evil eye"

### (27th May 1649)

(Written in phonetic Gaelic)

**90**

*"Cuirrith mi an obi er hull,*
*A hucht Phedir is Phoile,*
*An thia o neoth gi lar."*

*I will put an enchantment on the eye,*
*From the besom of Peter and Paul,*
*The one best Enchantment under the sun,*
*That will come from heaven to earth.*

---

George Black. *Witchcraft in Scotland*

## Bessie Smith's charm for Heart-fevers

### (1623)

Bessie Smith, the wise woman of Lasmahagow, was found gility of 'charming the heart feavers' (Rheumatic fever). She appointed them the Wayburne (plantain) leaf to be eaten nine mornings, and this charm be repeated, kneeling:

*For Godes sik,*
*For Sanct Spirit,*
*For Sanct Arkit,*
*For Nine Maidens that dyed*
*Into the Buirtie in the Ladywell bank,*
*This Charm to be beuk (book) and bell to me,*
*And that sua be.*

---

F. Marian McNeill. *The Silver Bough vol 1*

# Mary Steward's charm for migrantes
## (1705)

The wise woman of Kilbride in Arran confessed to the kirk that she used charms for heaing. An example of one of these charms is for curing migraines and "distempers in the head." The Gaelic charm goes as follows:

*Togidh criosd do chnamhan mar thog Muire a lamhan,*
*Nar thuireadh golann faoi nemh mar chruinnigh corp a chuimigh.*
*Togidh Peadar, togidh Pol, togidh Micheal, togidh Eoin,*
*Togidh Molais is Molinn cnamhan do chinn suas as an fheoil.*

**Translates:**

Chris will raise your bones as Mary raised her hands,

When she raised her eall of lementation towards heaven....

Peter raise up, Paul will raise, Michael will raise, John will raise,

Molaise and Moling will raise the bones of your head up out of the flesh.

---

Julian Goodare, Lauren Martin and Joyce Miller. *Witchcraft and Belieft in Early Modern Scortland*

# Jonet Anderson's charming of the Shirt

A common practice in Scotland for averting or curing illness was to charm a person's shirt instead of them being physically present during the rite. Jonet Anderson did this for a woman using the following incantation:

*Three bitter thingis hes thow bittin,*

*ill hart, ill ee, ill toung all meast;*
*uther three, may the beit,*
*the Father, the Sone, and Holy Ghost.*

**Translates:**

Three bitter things has thou been bitten,
Ill heart, Ill ear, Ill tongue all the most,
Other three, may it be,
The Father, The Son, and Holy Ghost

---

Pitcairn, Robert. *Ancient Criminal Trials in Scotland*

# OTHER SCOTTISH CHARMS
# AND SPELLS

*"With Sorcerie and Incantations,*
*Raising the Devill with invocationes,*
*With herbis, stanis, buiks and bellis,*
*Menis memberis and south-running wellis;*
*Palme-croces and knottis of strease,"*

Legend of the Bishop of St Androis

In this chapter I have compiled together spells and charms from all over Scotland. These spells and charms were mostly collected between the 18th and 20th centuries by folklorists interested in folk beliefs regarding magic and witchcraft, as well as other customs and traditions. Unlike those in the previous section, these spells and charms were not extracted from those who were convicted under the Witchcraft Acts in the previous centuries. In my opinion, since the practice of folk magic was no longer prohibited during this time, these spells and charms hold more authenticity as they were not tainted by possible false confession. Now this is not to say the oral collectors of these charms and spells were innocent of falsifying material, and I implore great caution regarding some early folklorists. Even Alexander Carmichael was guilty of altering the original transcripts in his final publication of the Carmina Gadelica for the sake of romanticization during the second wave of the Celtic Revival in Britain. For more information on this subject, consider my article *Alexander Carmichael: The Carmina Gadelica-shapring Scotland's Celtic Christianity* on my website.

To understand the magic of a charm or spell, I feel that we need to revisit the meaning of these words in their original context. In terms of popular magic today, is often thought of by common folk as simply a "lucky charm" sold on the roadside by fortune-tellers. However, this was not always the case and if we look further into the word's origins, we find it has a multi-magical meaning. In the Collins dictionary, the word 'charm' refers to an act, saying, or object believed to have magical powers. The word "charming" denotes the action while a "charmer" is the user of magical charms. To be "charmed" is to be blessed or divinely fortunate. "Even today a magical spell is used interchangeably with "charm." Spell comes from "spelling" or "to spell out," referring to a verbal formula belied to have magical force. In this book, I have used the word 'spell' in the original sense as an incantation where a ritual action was not required. Verbal charms would often be recited 3, 7, or 9 times according to Scottish folk magic, and often with each recitation getting louder and louder until ending in a shriek.

The application of a charm, as well as delivery of such, was magical in itself. Although charms would be simply spoken over the patient, written charms were also quite a popular way of delivering its magical effectiveness. These written charms were often placed into a small cloth bag and hung from the neck of a person or sewn into their clothing. There are some great examples of written charms such as two 19th century charms for toothaches from Ross-Shire. One of these charms was written and sold in 1855 by a professional witch named Kate McAulay who lived at Kishorn, Lochcarron. The other was given to a domestic servant in from Dingwall in 1869 by the wife of a gamekeeper at Garve. The written charm was to be folded seven or eight times and worn for at least a year in a small silk bag around the neck. It was also noted that the charm would lose its efficacy when others looked at it. Other applications of written charms included being placed in a bottle which was then bricked up in a wall or left in well water until diluted and then drunk by the patient. On few occasions, I have heard charms carved into a piece of cheese and consumed on a Sunday. In parts of Scotland, as well as practiced in Wales, charms recited or written back-wards would set about the reverse effects of the charm or a curse, the Lord's Prayer being the popular choice for deliberate diabolic magic.

In the highlands, black magic was known as *Cronachadh*, referring to acts of harm, ill-wishing, or cursing. White magic was known as *Beannachadh*, or blessing. A cure for an illness or against a curse was known as an *eolas* which came in a form of either spoken charm, magical action, or amulet. Charms and incantations can be divided into five classes. First, there are those for divination. Second, those which seek to attain certain ends. Third, those for protection. Fourth, those intended to cure men and beast of disease. Finally, there are those for blessing.

William Mackenzie (1895) gives details of all sorts of amulets, along with the five typical categories of charms within the Gaelic culture of Scotland:

> **Orr, orra, ortha**, or, as the Irish have it *ordid*. As the English word "charm" is derived from the Latin carmen, a song: and "incantation" from *cano*, I sing; so *orr* maybe derived from oro, I pray. The Irish *ordid* and the Latin *oratio* are probably different forms of the same word. In the Western Islands of Ireland, *ortha* means a hymn.
>
> **Orra-ghraidh**—An amulet to provoke unlawful love.
>
> **Orra-sheamlachais**—An amulet to make a cow allow the calf of another cow to suck her.
>
> **Orra-chomais**—An amulet to deprive a man of his virility, particularly on his marriage night, by way of vengeance.
>
> **Orra-na-h-aoine**—An amulet to drown a foe.
>
> **Orra an donuis**—An amulet to send one's foe to the mischief.
>
> **Orra-ghrudaire**—An amulet to make every drop of the wash to overflow the wash-tuns; and

***An orra-bhalbh***—An amulet to prevent one's agent
to make a defence in a court of justice.

In Scotland, same with many countries within Britain, there were four types of magical practitioners. The witch, wise woman, Charmer, and Fortune-teller/seer. The witch was deemed unlawful and used their powers for maleficia. The Wise Woman/Man used their powers to benefit themselves or community and would often counteract the witch's powers cast on their kin. The Charmer often just held one or two magical talents such as curing warts, burns, bone-setting, etc. Then there was the common fortune-teller, or seer, of the community who either told simple divination by cards, palmistry, or scrying. Seers may also have gained their foretelling abilities through second sight or being the seventh child of the seventh child. The term cunning-folk was not used in Scotland. Instead, terms such as canny or skeely man/woman were used in certain regions. By tradition, the charmer could only pass on their repertoire of magical charms contra-sexually, or woman to man and vice versa. However, if there was no predecessor of the opposite sex to be found, there was a wee loophole that the charmer could use in desperation. Charms would be taught to an inanimate object whilst the apprentice charmer would listen from another room or outside of an open window.

# Witchcraft, Spirits and the Second sight

## A Shetland rite in becoming a witch.

When the moon is full and at midnight, the aspirant after the unhallowed power goes alone to the seashore and lies down upon the black shore or below between the flood-tide mark. They then put their left hand under the soles of their feet and the right hand on the top of their head and intones, with great malediction:

*The Muckle maister deil tak' what's atween dis twa haunds.*

The devil will then appear and clenches the bargain or pact by the shaking of hands. When this is done there is no going back or retracting the pact with the devil. The person is his slave, and he gives her power on land and sea.

---

George. F Black. *County Folklore Vol. III Orkney & Shetland Islands*

## An Orkney rite in becoming a warlock.

This rite was performed by the soon-be witch with to procure the  powers of the warlock or witch. Mr Dennison wrote it down nearly 50 years ago from the recital of an old Orkney woman—the grand-daughter of a noted witch. The formula to be gone through to obtain witchcraft (or, as Mr Dennison says, in plain English, a formula for giving oneself to the Devil) was as follows:

While recording the rapidly

disappearing folklore and traditions of Sanday in the 1880s, folklorist Walter Traill Dennison documented the ritual carried out by aspiring witches to gain their magical powers. This rite was known as the 'Witch's Charm'.

The apprentice witch had to first wait for a full moon. Then she would go to a solitary beach at midnight where she had to turn widdershins (counter-clockwise) three times before lying prostrate on the ebb - the area between the limits of high and low tide.

She then had to stretch out her arms and legs, and place stones beside them. Further stones were also placed at her head, on her chest and over her heart.

Once enclosed by the circle of seven stones, the witch spoke aloud:

> O' Mester King o' a' that's ill,
> Come fill me wi' the Warlock Skill,
> An' I shall serve wi' all me will.
> Trow tak me gin I sinno!
> Trow tak me gin I winno!
> Trow tak me whin I cinno!
> Come tak me noo, an tak me a',
> Tak lights an' liver, pluck an' ga,
> Tak me, tak me, noo I say,
> Fae de how o' da heed, tae da tip o' da tae.
> Tak a' dats oot an' in o' me.
> Tak hare an hide an a' tae thee.
> Tak hert, an harns, flesh, bleud an banes,
> Tak a' atween the seeven stanes,
> I' de name o' da muckle black Wallowa!

**Translation:**

> Oh Master King of all that's ill,
> Come fill me with the Warlocks Skill
> And I shall serve [you] with all my will.

Trow take me if I sin!
Trow take me if I win!
Trow take me when I cannot!
Come take me now, and take me all,
Take eyes and liver, organs and feet
Take me, take me, now I say!
From the crown of the head, to the tip of the toe.
Take all that's out and in of me.
Take hair and hide and all to thee.
Take heart and brains, flesh, blood and bones
Take all between the seven stones!
In the name of the grand black Witch!

The person must lie quiet for a little time after repeating the Incantation. Then opening his eyes, he should turn on his left side, arise, and fling the stones used in the operation into the sea. Each stone must be flung singly; and with the throwing of each a certain malediction [unrecorded] was said.

Like the Orcadian scholar Hugh Marwick, I suspect elements of the rite - the ebb, the anticlockwise turns, and the positioning of the stones - represent an actual Orcadian tradition.

Certain lines, however, seem awkward and do not fit with the rest of the charm. Marwick believed some these may have been later additions, specifically added to impart an air of "evil" to the incantation. Marwick felt that the key to the charm lay in the lines:

*Tak me noo, an tak me a',*
*Tak lights an' liver, pluck an' ga',*
*Tak a' dats oot an' in o' me,*
*Tak hide an' hair an a' tae thee,*
*I' de nam o' de muckle black Wallowa!*

The oath sections calling upon the *trows* also seem at odds to the idea that the Incantation called upon the power of Satan - the Mester

King - so much so that Marwick suggested the first two lines were dramatic additions to an older charm, adding an association with the Devil that was never there in the original traditions. One question remains, however, and that is the identity of the "de muckle black Wallowa".

Although the word "Wallowa" or "Wallaway" is found in mainland Scottish dialect referring to the Devil, is seems more likely, given the other elements of the verse, that it is a corruption of a Norse term, "scotticised" into a word recognised by the recorder.

In this case we need look no further than the Old Norse "volva" - a prophetess or witch - a word whose Orcadian pronunciation could easily be mistaken for the Scots "Wallowa". Also, whats interesting and quite contradictory to this rite, that it is said that the 'Black Shore'—that is, the shore below the line or roll of seaweed thrown up by the tide, was sanctuary from all the supernatural beings that infest the night, for none dare go beyond the tide mark.

---

Marwick, Ernest W. *The Folklore Of Orkney And Shetland.*

*Okneyjar: the heritage of the Orkney islands* [online source]

F. Marian McNeill. *The Silver Bough vol. I*

## The Witch Cake

The baking of the 'Witch Cake' with its pernicious virtues, is a curious process, recorded in a traditional song, which we here give entire, to convince the fair reader that her lot is cast in safer times, when nature is the only tempter, and love the only Witch Cake:

*I saw yestreen, I saw yestreen,*
*Little wis ye what I saw yestreen,*
*The black cat pyked out the gray ane's een,*
*At the hip o' the hemlock knowe yestreen.*
*Wi' her tail i' her teeth she whomel'd roun',*

*Wi' her tail i' her teeth she whomel'd roun',*
*Till a braw star drapt frae the lift aboon,*
*An' she keppit it e'er it wan to the grun'.*
*She hynt them a' in her mow' an' chowed,*
*She hynt them a' in her mow' an' chowed,*
*She drabbled them owre wi' a black tade's blude,*
*An' baked a bannock, - an' ca'd it gude! -*
*She haurned it weel wi' ae blink o' the moon,*
*She haurned it weel wi' ae blink o' the moon,*
*An withre-shines thrice she whorled it roun',*
*There's some sall skirl ere ye be done.*
*Some Lass maun gae wi' a kilted sark,*
*Some priest maun preach in a thackless kirk;*
*Thread maun be spun for a dead man's sark,*
*A' maun be done e'er the sang o' the lark.*
*Tell nae what ye saw yestreen,*
*Tell nae what ye saw yestreen,*
*There's ane may gaur ye sich an graen,*
*For telling what ye saw yestreen!*

---

Robert Hartley Cromek. *Remains of Nithsdale and Galloway song*

## A Witches Reel

The witches of North Berwick (1590) were said to have danced to a hypnotic tune and song around the kirk near the shore. Original the witches were recorded to have sung: "*Cummer gae ye before, cummer gae ye. Gin ye winna gae before, cummer let me*" only, but F. Marian McNeill had later extended the verses in the chant which has come to be popularly known as:

*Cummer gae ye before, cummer gae ye,*
*Gin ye winna gae before, cummer let me,*
*Ring-a-ring-a-widdershins*
*Linkin lithely widdershins,*
*Cummers carlin cron and queyn*

**103**

*Roun gae we!*

*Cummer gae ye before, cummer gae ye,*
*Gin ye winna gae before, cummer let me,*
*Ring-a-ring-a-widdershins*
*Loupin' lightly widdershins,*
*Kilted coats and fleein' hair*
*Three times three!*

*Cummer gae ye before, cummer gae ye,*
*Gin ye winna gae before, cummer let me,*
*Ring-a-ring-a-widdershins*
*Whirlin' skirlin' widdershins,*
*De'il tak the hindmost*
*Wha'er she be!*

I have had many of fond memories with friends spinning faster and faster nine times in a circle holding hands to Green Crown's rendition of this chant titled 'The Witches Reel'. However, this can be used by people who practice Traditional Witchcraft to *'Tread the Mill'* or Compass round for the trance-like effects it has after it is performed. There is also a traditional Scottish dance known as the 'Witches Reel' which can be seen on YouTube.

---

Thomas Davidson. *Rowan tree and Red Thread'*

## The *Hairy-tedder*

A *hairy-tedder/tether* or known simply as a witch's rope was made of the hairs drawn from the tail of every cow within reach and tugging on the ripe whilst muttering an incantation had the power to draw all the milk from their neighbour's cow to her own pail. The witch of Carse of Gowrie, it is said, was seen pulling at a Hairy-tether along which streams of milk were flowing, and heard repeating this incantation:

*Mare's milk and deer's milk,*
*And every beast that bears milk,*
*Atween st. Johnson and Dundee,*
*Come a' to me, come a' to me!*

A Shetlander once watched a witch at her work of "taking the profit" from her neighbour's cows. She had collected all the cow's tethers and had tied them to a stake hammered into the ground. With the loose ends of the tethers in her hand, she ran around in the circle, saying as she ran:

*By da crap o' da hedder,*
*An' da black bull's bleddder,*
*In da circle o' dis tedder*
*Be da luck o' a' man's hoose*
*An' a' sort o' produce.*
*Dat is o' ony use-*
*An' a ta me, an a' ta me*

The watcher shouted, 'An' pairt ta me, Luckie'. When he got home, he found his sister standing beside her churn with a frightened look on her face. She said that so butter had come into the *kirn* (churn) that she did not know what to do with it.

I have made and used a *hairy-tether* myself to help people tame and control unruly pets by having the person comb their dog or cat and get as much hair as they can in a space of a week. Then, with black wool and the use of sugared water, I have twined the pet's fur around the clew, whilst saying an adaptation of the 'Twist ye, twine ye' charm (see **miscellaneous**). One can also adapted the incantation above if you so wish in using the *Hairy-tether* in this way.

---

F. Marian McNeill. *The Silver Bough vol. I*

Earnest W. Marwick. *The Folklore of Orkney and Shetland*

# To see what the seer sees

The usual Method for a curious Person to get a transient Sight of this otherwise invisible Crew of Subterranean, (if impotently and over rashly sought,) is to put his left Foot under the Wizard's right Foot, and the Seer's Hand is put on the Inquirer's Head, who is to look over the Wizard's right Shoulder, which his ane ill Appearance, as if by this Ceremony an implicit Surrender were made of all betwixt the Wizard's Foot and his Hand, ere the Person can be admitted a privado to the Airt; then will he see a Multitude of Wight's, like furious hardy Men, flocking to him hastily from all Quarters, as thick as Atoms in the Air.

---

Robert Kirk. *The Secret Commonwealth of Elves, Fauns and Fairies*

# To receive a vision in your sleep

This magical formula is most effective when performed on *samhainn* or Hallowmas if a woman wanted to receive a vision of something, most likely who her future husband will be. On the evening, a young woman was to go to a Boundary Stream (*allt crìche*), (between two neighbouring proprietors the better) and with closed eyes, lifted from it three stones between the middle finger and thumb, saying these words:

> *"I will lift the stone*
> *As Mary lifted it for her Son,*
> *For substance, virtue, and strength;*
> *May this stone be in my hand*
> *Till I reach my journey's end."*

The stones were for putting under the head (pillow) when going to sleep. In Scottish folk magic, stones used in magical applications were often of white, black, and red, or even white stones like other dreaming stones that were used in parts of Britain. Also, although the formula denotes a woman was to perform the rite, I see no reason why a man could not perform it.

---

Campbell, John Gregorson. *Witchcraft and Second Sight*

## A seer's charm for seeing fairies or spirits of the Dead

A Man with the Privileges of the whole Mystery of this Second Sight wish to see spirits or fairies at will. He must run a Tedder (rope) made of hair which has been bound the Corps to the Bier, in a Helix (wrapped a number of times) about his middle (waist), from End to End; then bow his Head downwards, as did Elijah, (*1 Kings, 18. 42.*) did, and look back through his Legs until he sees a Funeral advance till the people cross two Marches; or look thus back through a Hole where was a Knot (crevice) of Fir [wood], But if the wind change points while the Hair Tedder is tied about him, he is in peril of his life.

---

Robert Kirk. *The Secret Commonwealth of Elves, Fauns and Fairies*

## The *Taghairm*: a Scottish necromancy ritual

The *Taghairm*, or "spirit-calling" is a term referred to two rites within Gaelic mysticism, the one being a necromantic rite to call up spirits of the dead for advice or prophecy. The second, known as *Taghairm nan Caht*, being a gruesome ritual of being granted second sight, magical powers, or otherworldly knowledge by the means of roasting live cats, one after another. As such, the early folklorist Martin Martin was the first to record the rites referred to as the Taghairm, and describes the seer or wise man performing the rite, in having:

retired to solitary places, remote from any house, and there they singled out one of their number, and wrapped him in a big Cows Hide which they folded about him, his whole Body was covered with it except his head, and so left in this posture all night until his invisible friends (spirits relieved him, by giving a proper answer to the question in hand, which he received, as he fancied, from several persons that he found about him all that time, his consorts returned to him at break of Day, and then he communicated his news to them, which often proved fatal to those concerned in such unwarrantable inquiries.

This rite that Martin Martin mentions here, was often performed by the local wise man or man of second sight, with the help of his ghostly friends, in the intention of receiving future outcomes of severe events such as war, death, sickness etc. The second rite, although unrelated to the first, is the *Taghairm nan Chat* or the spirit-call of the cat:

There was a third way of consulting, which was a confirmation of the second abovementioned. The same company who put the man into the hide, took a live cat, and put him on a spit, one of the Number was employed to turn the spit, and one of his consorts enquired at him, what are you doing? He answered, I roast this cat, until his (ghostly) friends answer the question, which must be the game that was proposed by the man shut up in the hide, and afterwards a very big cat comes attended by a number of lesser cats, desiring to relieve the cat turned on the spit, and then answers the question: If this Answer prove the same that was given to the man in the Hide, then it was taken as a confirmation of the other which in this case was believed infallible.

In later folklore, it mentions that the otherworldly cat was referred to as the *cat-sìth* or the fairy cat, or in other areas as simply being "big ears". This demon-like cat was invoked by the live sacrifice of the spirit's feline companions until the demon-cat could stand it no more. The fairy cat or "big ears" was said to have the powers to bestow upon the applicants of this rite the powers of second sight, witch's powers, or otherworldly knowledge.

Although I wouldn't recommend the modern practitioners perform *Taghairm nan Chat* for obvious reasons, the Taghairm as rite of spirit communication or travel, can quite possibility be adapted to the needs of the modern practitioner. Although in some sources the rite demands a freshly culled hide of a cow or bull be used, I have used an antique cow hide which I have marked with signs and symbols associated with the dead and the "Otherworld". Such as the skull and crossed bones, scythe or sickle, or an image of the grave, coffin, or burial mound, in order aid the death-like trance needed for the communication of certain spirits summoned in Taghairm oracle.

---

Martin Martin. *A Description of the Western Islands of Scotland*

## To summon the spirits of the *Airts*

Within Scots language, there is two meanings to the word *Airt*, one meaning art such as the 'black airts' and the other, which is used here, is to refer to the cardinal points, seasons and the circulation either clockwise or counter-clockwise. which could refer to the Eastern star and the nativity of Jesus Christ. This incantation chanted by the witches in Shakespeare's Macbeth utilised the Airts in both the sense of the spirits of north, east, south, and east, and the act of circulation:

> *Black spirits and white, red spirits and grey,*
> *Mingle, mingle, mingle, you that mingle may.*
> *Titty, Tiffin, keep it stiff in.*
> *Firedrake, Puckey, make it lucky.*

**109**

*Liard, Robin, you must bob in.*
*Round, around, around, about, about,*
*All ill come running in, all good keep out.*

**Alternative:**

*Black spirits, white,*
*Red spirits, gray,*
*Come ye, come ye*
*Come what may.*

*Around and round,*
*Throughout, about.*
*The good stay in.*
*The ill keep out.*

The enchanter is intended to circle around a space or object which invokes the aid of the spirits of the four cardinal points. Some traditional witches in Scotland use this chant in "treading the mill" or compass-round. Some scholars attest that *airt* came from the Gàidhlig word *'ear'* for east. As an old Scottish proverb says, *"Evil never came from the East"*, and within Scottish folk magic a circulation begins at the east for good and south for ill. The correspondence for the *Airts* goes as follows:

**Ear** (East)- red spirits, spring, dawn, fire, lightening, the *deiseil* turn (clockwise)

**Deas** (south)-black spirits, summer, noon, earth, earthquakes

**Iar** (west)- Grey spirits, autumn, twilight, water, rain

**Tuath** (north) white spirits, winter, midnight, snow, the *tuaithiuil* or *widdershins* turn (counterclockwise)

---

F. Marian McNeill. *The Silver Bough vol. I*

Notes to *Macbeth*, Act 4, Scene 1, line 39:"Black spirits, etc. [online source]

# Curses, hexes and other harmful magic

## The Wicked who would do me harm

### (*ulc a dhean mo lochd*)

This charm was obtained from Isabella Chisholm from Alexander Carmichael in the 1890's. Carmichael notes that "she had the gipsy habits and the gipsy language, variously called 'Cant,' 'Shelta,' 'Romany,' with rich fluent Gaelic and English. She had many curious spells, runes, and hymns". This charm is what I class as the psalm 109 of Gaelic curses, where it is used to cause severe harm to a wicked person you intend to smite:

*Ulc a dhean mo lochd*
*Gun gabh e 'n galar gluc gloc,*
*Guirneanach, gioirneanach, guairneach,*
*Gaornanach, garnanach, gruam.*

*Gum bu cruaidhe c na chlach,*
*Gum bu duibhe e na 'n gual,*
*Gum bu luaithe e na 'n lach,*
*Gum bu truime e na 'n luaidh.*

*Gum bu gointe, gointe, geuire, gairbhe, guiniche e,*
*Na'n cuilionn cruaidh cnea-chridheach,*
*Gum bu gairge e na'n salann sion, sionn, searbh, sailte,*
*Seachd seachd uair.*

The wicked who would do me harm
May he take the [throat] disease,
Globularly, spirally, circularly,
Fluxy, pellety, horny-grim.

Be it harder than the stone,
Be it blacker than the coal,
Be it swifter than the duck,
Be it heavier than the lead.

Be it fiercer, fiercer, sharper,
harsher, more malignant,
Than the hard, wound-quivering holly,
Be it sourer than the sained,
lustrous, bitter, salt salt,
Seven seven times.

Oscillating thither,

*A turabal a null,*
*A tarabal a nall,*
*A treosdail a sios,*
*A dreochail a suas,*

*A breochail a muigh,*
*A geochail a staigh,*
*Dol a mach minic,*
*Tighinn a steach ainmic.*

Undulating hither,
Staggering downwards,
Floundering upwards.

Drivelling outwards,
Snivelling inwards,
Oft hurrying out,
Seldom coming in.

*Sop an luib gach laimhe,*
*Cas an cois gach cailbhe,*
*Lurg am bun gach ursann,*
*Sput ga chur 's ga chairbinn.*

A wisp the portion of each hand,
A foot in the base of each pillar,
A leg the prop of each jamb,
A flux driving and dragging him.

*Gearrach fhala le cridhe, le crutha,*
*le cnamha,*
*Le gruthan, le sgumhan, le sgamha,*
*Agus sgrudadh cuisil, ugan is arna,*
*Dha mo luchd-tair agus tallies.*

A dysentery of blood from heart,
from form, from bones,
From the liver, from the lobe, from
the lungs,
And a searching of veins, of throat,
and of kidneys,
To my contemners and traducers.

*An ainm Dhia nam feart,*
*A shiab uam gach olc,*
*'S a dhion mi le neart,*
*Bho lion mo luchd-freachd*
*Agus fuathachd.*

In name of the God of might,
Who warded from me every evil,
And who shielded me in strength,
From the net of my breakers
And destroyers.

---

Alexander Carmichael. *Carmina Gadelica, Vol II*

# The Border Reivers Cursing Stone

In 1525 the reivers had become such a nuisance that the then Archbishop of Glasgow, Gavin Dunbar, put a curse up all the reivers of the borderlands.

*"I curse their head and all the hairs of their head; I curse their face, their brain (innermost thoughts), their mouth, their nose, their tongue, their teeth, their forehead, their shoulders, their breast, their heart, their stomach, their back, their womb, their arms, their leggs, their hands, their feet, and every part of their body, from the top of their head to the soles of their feet, before and behind, within and without."*

*"I curse them going and I curse them riding; I curse them standing and I curse them sitting; I curse them eating and I curse them drinking; I curse them rising, and I curse them lying; I curse them at home, I curse them away from home; I curse them within the house, I curse them outside of the house; I curse their wives, their children, and their servants who participate in their deeds. I (bring ill wishes upon) their crops, their cattle, their wool, their sheep, their horses, their swine, their geese, their hens, and all their livestock. I (bring ill wishes upon) their halls, their chambers, their kitchens, their stanchions, their barns, their cowsheds, their barnyards, their cabbage patches, their plows, their harrows, and the goods and houses that are necessary for their sustenance and welfare."*

*"May all the malevolent wishes and curses ever known, since the beginning of the world, to this hour, light on them. May the malediction of God, that fell upon Lucifer and all his fellows, that cast them from the high Heaven to the deep hell, light upon them."*

*"May the fire and the sword that stopped Adam from the gates of Paradise, stop them from the glory of Heaven, until they forebear, and make amends."*

*"May the evil that fell upon cursed Cain, when he slew his brother Abel, needlessly, fall on them for the needless slaughter that they commit daily."*

*"May the malediction that fell upon all the world, man and beast, and all that ever took life, when all were drowned by the flood of Noah, except Noah and his ark, fall upon them and drown them, man and beast, and make this realm free of them, for their wicked sins."*

*"May the thunder and lightning which rained down upon Sodom and Gomorra and all the lands surrounding them, and burned them for their vile sins, rain down upon them and burn them for their open sins. May the evil and confusion that fell on the Gigantis for their opression and pride in building the Tower of Babylon, confound them and all their works, for their open callous disregard and opression."*

*"May all the plagues that fell upon Pharoah and his people of Egypt, their lands, crops and cattle, fall upon them, their equipment, their places, their lands, their crops and livestock."*

*"May the waters of the Tweed and other waters which they use, drown them, as the Red Sea drowned King Pharoah and the people of Egypt, preserving God's people of Israel."*

*"May the earth open, split and cleave, and swallow them straight to hell, as it swallowed cursed Dathan and Abiron, who disobeyed Moses and the command of God."*

*"May the wild fire that reduced Thore and his followers to two-hundred-fifty in number, and others from 14,000 to 7,000 at anys, usurping against Moses and Aaron, servants of God, suddenly burn and consume them daily, for opposing the commands of God and Holy Church."*

*"May the malediction that suddenly fell upon fair Absolom, riding through the wood against his father, King David, when the branches of a tree knocked him from his horse and hanged him by the hair, fall upon these untrue Scotsmen and hang them the same way, that all the world may see."*

*"May the malediction that fell upon Nebuchadnezzar's lieutenant, Olifernus, making war and savagery upon true christian men; the malediction that fell upon Judas, Pilate, Herod, and the Jews that crucified Our Lord; and all the*

**114**

*plagues and troubles that fell on the city of Jerusalem therefore, and upon Simon Magus for his treachery, bloody Nero, Ditius Magcensius, Olibrius, Julianus Apostita and the rest of the cruel tyrants who slew and murdered Christ's holy servants, fall upon them for their cruel tyranny and murder of Christian people."*

*"And may all the vengeance that ever was taken since the world began, for open sins, and all the plagues and pestilence that ever fell on man or beast, fall on them for their openly evil ways, senseless slaughter and shedding of innocent blood."*

*"I sever and part them from the church of God, and deliver them immediately to the devil of hell, as the Apostle Paul delivered Corinth. I bar the entrance of all places they come to, for divine service and ministration of the sacraments of holy church, except the sacrament of infant baptism, only; and I forbid all churchmen to hear their confession or to absolve them of their sins, until they are first humbled / subjugated by this curse."*

*"I forbid all christian men or women to have any company with them, eating, drinking, speaking, praying, lying, going, standing, or in any other deed-doing, under the pain of deadly sin."*

*"I discharge all bonds, acts, contracts, oaths, made to them by any persons, out of loyalty, kindness, or personal duty, so long as they sustain this cursing, by which no man will be bound to them, and this will be binding on all men."*

*"I take from them, and cast down all the good deeds that ever they did, or shall do, until they rise from this cursing."*

*"I declare them excluded from all matins, masses, evening prayers, funerals or other prayers, on book or bead (rosary); of all pigrimages and alms deeds done, or to be done in holy church or be christian people, while this curse is in effect."*

*"And, finally, I condemn them perpetually to the deep pit of hell, there to remain with Lucifer and all his fellows, and their bodies to the gallows of Burrow moor, first to be hanged, then ripped and torn by dogs, swine, and other wild beasts, abominable to all the world. And their candle (light of their life) goes from*

**115**

*your sight, as may their souls go from the face of God, and their good reputation*
*from the world, until they forebear their open sins, aforesaid, and rise from this*
*terrible cursing and make satisfaction and penance."*

In the year 2000 a stone commemorating the Monition of Cursing was erected in Carlisle, Cumbria near to the formidable pile that is Carlisle castle. The words of the curse is engraved on this giant stone, going around in a way that that the reader has to walk widdershins (anti-clockwise) around it. But residents in Carlisle claim the stone have brought them disasters from disease to the relegation of the local soccer team.

In 2005 Carlisle was overtaken by floods of an unprecedented level. Houses were swamped to their upper floors as the river Eden burst its banks and engulfed everything in its path. Vast swathes of the city were underwater for days, houses on the flood plain of the river seriously damaged. Many had to leave their homes and find shelter elsewhere for up to and over a year before they could return. It was an extremely harrowing episode in the history of this proud northern place just south of the Border with Scotland.

Also, only weeks after the oval-shaped stone was installed, foot and mouth saw one half of Cumbria's livestock burning on funeral pyres, followed by a succession of factory closures and relegation for Carlisle United.

The curse was taken so seriously that a Council member proposed the removal of the stone.
The city council took advice from local Christian groups, including the Bishop of Carlisle and a blessing was included within the artwork taken from The Bible, Philippians 4 Verse 6 to try and counteract the curse.

ScotClans: Scottish clans. *The Border Reivers Cursing Stone* (2018). [online source]

# The Clay Doll

## (Corp Creadh)

The greatest evil that witches can do is to make, for a person whose death they desire, a clay body or image (corp creadha), into which pins are stuck, to produce a slow and painful disease, terminating in dissolution. Waxen figures for the same purpose, and melted by exposure to a slow fire, were known to Lowland superstition. In the Highlands wax was not accessible to poor bodies, and they had to make clay serve the turn. It is said that when a person wants a limb he cannot be destroyed by witches in this manner.

When the *corp chre* or *Corp Creadh* is made ready for receiving the pins, the operator addresses it in this manner: "*'s cosmhal thu o d'chulaobh ri reithe air am bitheadh sean ruisg*" (from behind you are like a ram with an old fleece). As the pins are being put in, a long incantation is used, the beginning of which is something to this effect: "*mar a cnamhas thusa, gu cnamhadh ise: mar leonas so thusa, gu leonadh ise*" (as you waste away may she waste away, as this wounds you may it wound-her). If the *Corp-creadh*, be a clay image it was usually deposited in a running stream. As the action of the water gradually dissolved it, the person it represented slowly and painfully wasted away. The wax image would be placed beside the fire, slowly to dissolved, and as it melted away, the life of the person it was desired to injure gradually ebbed.

---

R. C. Maclagan. *Notes on Folklore Objects Collected in Argyleshire*

John Gregorson Campbell. *Witchcraft & second sight in the Highlands & Islands*

# The Witch's Cursing Bone

As was this cursing bone, fixed through a diamond-shaped piece of bog wood. It belonged to a reputed witch in Glen Shira at Inveraray in Argyll who supposedly used it to 'ill-will' people in the community.

According to a local tradition collected by Lady Elspeth Campbell, the blood of a newly killed hen was poured through the bone as a curse was spoken.

The bone is the thigh bone of a deer or sheep, fixed through a naturally formed, diamond-shaped piece of bog oak (in which a knot has left a hole). This charm can be seen displayed at the National Museum of Scotland which if you are unable to attend in-person, can be viewed online on their website.

F. Marion McNeill. *The Silver Bough Vol I*

National Museum of Scotland Blog- https://blog.nms.ac.uk/

## To render an enemy deaf

A highland clansman would hold a churchyard yew sprig in his hand when denouncing or threatening an enemy. This made his challenge inaudible; his victim could hear nothing, but other witnesses could. The attacker would insist that he had made his intentions plain, there was no treachery, and still retains the advantage of surprises attack.

Margaret Back. *Discovering the Folklore of Plants*

## A Malediction

### (mallachd)

A charm simply titled *Mallachd*, or a Malediction used to curse both man and beast:

> *Thaining dithis a mach*
> *A Cathrach Neobh,*
> *Fear agus bean,*
> *A dheanadh nan öisnean.*

*Mallaich dha na beana bur-shuileach,*
*Mallaich dha na feara fur-shuileach,*
*Mallaich dha na ceithir saighde, guineach, guid,*
*Dh' fhaodadh a bhi 'n aorabh duin's bruid*

**Translates:**

There came two out
From the City of Heaven,
A man and a woman,
To make the 'ōisnean.'

Curses on the blear-eyed women,
Curses on the sharp-eyed men,
Curses on the four venomous arrows of disease,
That may be in the constitution of man and beast.

Alexander Carmichael. *Carmina Gadelica, Vol II*

# A medieval book Curse

Write this verse on the first page of your book and it will bring about a curse on anyone who steals it, borrows it without your permission, or does not return it to you:

*For him that stealeth, or borroweth and returneth not, this book from its owner, let it change into a serpent in his hand & rend him. Let him be struck with palsy & all his members blasted. Let him languish in pain crying aloud for mercy, & let there be no surcease to his agony till he sing in dissolution. Let bookworms gnaw his entrails in token of the Worm that dieth not, & when at last he goeth to his final punishment, let the flames of Hell consume him for ever*

**119**

**Another:**

# The Evil Eye, Unbewitching and Protection

## The Fiery Circle or Blessing of the circle
### (Beannachadh na Cuairte)

A curious fire rite known as the Fiery Circle or *Beannachadh na Cuairte*, the blessing of the circle was used to by a wise person of the community for dwindling or sick children, to counteract the 'evil eye' that was responsible for its condition. An iron hoop was procured- often the hoop that encircled the wash-tub- and round it but leaving a space at each side of the diameter for the hand to grasp, the wise women and/or men of the district wound a *siaman* or straw rope.

Then, having saturate it with paraffin oil, they set it on fire. The hoop was held vertically by the two other people, and the 'wise woman or man' passed the chid through the blazing circle (often three, seven or nine times), using the appropriate incantation. Although the incantation was not mentioned, here is one that might be sufficient use due to the fact it may be associated with the number of (seven) times the child to be passed through the fiery circle: -

*Co a thilleas cronachduinn suil?*
*Tillidh mise tha mi 'n duil,*
*Ann an ainm Righ nan dul.*
*Tri seachd gairmeachdain co ceart,*
*Labhair Criosd an dorusd na cathrach;*
*Paidir Moire a h-aon,*
*Paidir Righ a dha,*
*Paidir Moire a tri,*
*Paidir Righ a ceithir,*
*Paidir Moire a coig,*
*Paidir Righ a sia,*
*Paidir Moire a seachd;*
*Tillidh seachd paidrichean Moire*
*Cronachduinn suil,*
*Co dhiubh bhitheas e air duine no air bruid,*
*Air mart no air earc;*
*Thusa bhi na d' h-ioma shlainte nochd,*
*[An t-ainm]*
*An ainm an Athar, a Mhic, 's an Spioraid Naoimh. Amen*

**Translates:**

Who shall thwart the evil eye?
I shall thwart it, methinks,
In name of the King of life.
Three seven commands so potent,
Christ Spoke at the door of the city;
Pater Mary one,
Pater King two,

Pater Mary three,
Pater King four,
Pater Mary five,

**121**

Pater King six,
Pater Mary seven;
Seven pater Maries will thwart
The evil eye,
Whether it be on man or on beast,
On horse or on cow;
Be thou in thy full health this night,
[patient's name]
In name of the Father, the Son, and the Holy Spirit. Amen

F. Marion McNeill. *The Silver Bough Vol I*

Alexander Carmichael. *Carmina Gadelica, Vol II*

## To protect doors and gates from Evil

To protect doors and gates from the Dark Master you must say over the thresholds:

*With Hurt and hate*
*I charm this gate*
*He shall not sleep too soon or late.*

To life the charm put on the gate or doors, the following must be chanted in a low clear voice:

*I take the spell from off this gate*
*Nae ill shall fall o' muckle hate,*
*Till the devil speaks the world of fate,*
*Hail shall he be in the devil's name.*

Cameron, Isabel; *Highland Chapbook*

# A water rite for the Evil Eye

With a crock of clay or a small wooden clog the healer went to a running stream and stopped at the place where the dead and the living cross*. She or he spoke to no living prson from the side of the bridge or ford, she went down on her right knee, lifted as much water as she could in her cupped hands, and poured it into the crock, repeating the rune (ran):

*Tha mi togail boinnein bùrn*
*An aimn nùmh an Athair,*
*An aimn nùmh a' Mhic,*
*An ainm nùmh Spioraid.*
I am lifting a little drop of water

In the name of the father,
In the holy name of the son,
In the holy name of the spirit.

On returning to the house [of the patient], she sprinkled some of the water in the ears and along the spine of the person or animal on whom the Evil Eye had rested, pronouncing his name, and repeating these words:

*Crath dhìot do dìth,*
*Crath dhìot do ghnù,*
*Crath dhìot do dhosgaidh.*
*An aimn Athir,*
*An aimn Mic,*
*An aimn spiorad Nùmh.*

Shake from thee thy harm,
Shake from thee thy jealously,
Shake from thee thy illness,
In the name of the Father,
In the name of the Son,
In the name of the Holy Spirit.

**123**

The remainder of the water was poured on to a grey stone, or a fixed rock that fails not, or behind the fire-flag (hearth stone).

Interestingly, a rhyme denotes the fire-flag as being the completion in healing sick animals/persons and destroyed the force of the Evil Eye:

*Thy strait be on the fire-flags,*

*Thine ailment on the wicked woman.*

---

F. Marian McNeill. *The Silver Bough vol. I*

Ann Ross. *Folklore of the Scottish Highlands*

## Recollections of Practices formerly used to avert and avoid the power of Witchery.

Having a small, smooth limestone, picked up on the beach, with its edges rubbed down by friction and the continual action of the sea, and with a natural hole through it, tied to the key to a house, ware-house, barn, stable, or other building, prevented the influence of witches over whatever the house, &c. Contained.

Sailors nailed a horseshoe on the foremast, and jockeys one on the stable door, but to be effective the shoe ought necessarily to be found by accident.

On meeting a suspected witch, the thumb of each hand was turned inward, and the fingers firmly closed upon it; care was also taken to let her have the wall-side or best path.

Caution was used that glove, or any portion of apparel worn next to the skin, came not into the possession of a witch, as it was strongly believed she had a highly ascendant power over the rightful owner.

A bit of witch-wood, or a hare's foot, was carried in the pocket, under an impression that the possessor was free from any harm that otherwise might accrue from the old hag's malignant practices.

One thing of importance was not to go out of the house in a morning without taking a bite of bread, cake, or other eat- able to break the fast.

A thick white curtain was hung inside the window, to prevent an 'evil eye' being cast into the room.

If a few drops of the old creature's blood could be obtained, they were considered sufficiently efficacious in preventing her 'secret, black, and baneful workings.'

Although the practices abovementioned are spoken of in the past tense, they are not, at the present time, altogether done away; not a few, who are now living, are credulous enough to believe in their potency. The following may be mentioned as a fact, which occurred a short time ago in the neighbourhood where the writer of this article resides: - A person bought a pig, which after keeping for some time 'grew very badly,' and witchery was suspected to be the cause; to ascertain the certainty of the fact nine buds of the elder- tree (here commonly called buttery) were laid in a straight line, and all pointing one way; a dish made of ash-wood was inverted and placed carefully over them, and left to the next morning. This was done under an idea that if the pig were bewitched the buds would be found in disorder, but if not, in the state in which they were originally left.

Four plants which are was said to combat witches, as this rhyme run: -

*Trefoil, Vervain, John's wort, Dill,*
*Hinders witches in their will.*

In the past I have used all four plants in creating a powder or charm bag to ward or break a witch's spell set upon me.

T. C. Bridlington, July 30, 1827
F. Marian McNeill. *The Silver Bough Vol. I*

## The Threefold charm against all evil

As illustrated at the beginning of this chapter, where a cross of Rowan, a horseshoe and a St. John's wort are known as the "Threefold charm" against all evil and witchcraft.

In Tiree a person lost several stirks by the stakes falling and strangling them in the byre. A 'wise' woman, reputed a witch, advised, though her advice was not taken, that the *right-hand part of a fore horse-shoe, with three nails in it*, should be put below the threshold (*stairsneach*) of the byre, along with a silver coin, and that the hind quarter of one of the beasts should be taken *west* and buried beyond the limits of the farm. This was to prevent a similar calamity in future.

M.B. J. Maxwell Wood. *Witchcraft and Superstitious Record in South-Western District of Scotland*

## Rowan wood and Red Thread

As a protection of man and beast against the witch's power, the rowan or mountain ash was the first to be used as a ward. This practice was nearly allied to one which was very prevalent, and of which some traces still exist in what would be esteemed a more enlightened part of the world, i.e., wearing a small piece of the branch of the rowan tree wrapped around with red thread and sewed into some parts of the garments, to guard against the effects of the evil eye or witchcraft:

> 'Rowan tree and red thread
> Will drive the witches a' wud.'

Or another verse has it as:

> A Rowan-tree and a red thread
> Gars a' the witches dance to dead.

Several rhymes have been recorded that show just how widespread the belief in the powers of the Rowan charm was:

*Rowan-tree and red thread*
*Make the witches tyne their speed.*

From the Borders of Scotland:

*Black luggie, lammer bead,*
*Rowan-tree and red thread,*
*Put the witches to their speed!*

Or, from the north-east of Scotland:

*The rawn-tree in the widd-bin*
*Hand the witches on cum in.*

Around Lùnastal, the berries of the rowan tree were often collected and then dried so that they could be strung together on a red thread and worn as a necklace for protection. Red coral or amber, strung on red silk, were often used as a substitue for rowan by those of greater financial means. According to Maclagan, ripe rowan berries (*caorain dearg*) were often kept close to hand "as sufficient to prevent any injury coming to him from the Evil Eye or Witchcraft.

---

**Note:** *Black luggie*, a Scottish two-handled drinking cup and *lammer* is Amber.

J. M. McPherson. *Primitive Beliefs in the North-East of Scotland*

Ellen Emma Guthrie. *Old Scottish Customs: Local and General*

# A Grand rite for unbewitching

A woman who suspected that her cows had been witched repaired to march between two lairds (lords) lands and pull fifteen green nettles by the roots. These were bound in a sheaf and placed on the *looder* of a watermill.

Then the woman, providing herself with a triangular clipping of *Skrootie Claith* (orange cloth), two *Noralegs*\*, a flint and steel, and a box of tinder, went to the mill at the hour of midnight, and taking the bundle of nettles, wended her way to the kirkyard of the parish. Arriving there, she went to the east side of the yard, and crossed the dyke (stream) back foremost.

Selecting an open, the nettles are unloosed, and twelve of the number are placed end to end, to form a circle.
They are counted out backwards, while the following formula is slowly repeated:

> "*Da twal, da twal Apostles;*
> *Da 'leven, da 'leven Evangelists;*
> *Da ten, da ten Commandments;*
> *Da nine, da brazen shiners;*
> *Da eight, da holy waters;*
> *Da seven, da stars o' heaven;*
> *Da six, Creation's dawnin;*
> *Da five, da timblers o' da bools;*
> *Da four, da gospel makers;*
> *Da tree, da triddle treevers;*
> *Da twa lily white boys that clothe themselves*
> *In green;*
> *Da een, da een dat walks alon', an' evermore*
> *Sall rue*"

Two of the remaining three nettles are now placed in the centre of the circle in the form of a St. Andrew's cross. The two *Noralegs* are also stuck into the *claith* (cloth) in the form of a cross. Then with the *noralegs* in one hand and the odd nettle in the other, she takes her stand within the sacred circle and exclaims:

*"With this green nettle*
*And cross of metal*
*I witches and wierds defy;*
*O' walds's gear gi'e me na mair*
*Than the luck back ta da kye.*
*Whae'ver it be, else he or she,*
*In sorrow may dey live an' dee,*
*In porta may dey pine."*

**Translated:**

With this green nettle
And cross of metal
The witches and weirds defy,
Of the world's goods go with me more
Then the luck go back to the kye.
Whatever it be, else he or she,
In sorrow may they live and be,
In porta may they pine.

The, suiting the action to the word, she sets fire to tinder, saying: "So perish all my foes."

This wierd (weird) performance is now over, the nettles are collected, and the woman returns to her home in the small hours of the morning. The nettles are buried in the *gulgraave o' da vyaedie* (open drain) of the byre. The *noralegs* are stuck into the byre wall near the *vagil baand* *of the cow, and as both rotted and corroded, so the witch was supposed to be seized with some wasting disease.

Although this charm is used to on bewitched cattle, I can be used to for yourself or another person, by striking the *Noralegs* into the frame of you bed or front door and having the nettles buried under your threefold or near your home. The first incantation, I have also used when tying the nine-knotted clew *see miscellaneous.*

---

Notes: * *looder;* A heavy wooden bar or pole used for levering up a millstone.
*noralegs;* a large pin, an awl, or needle, often with a broken eye. * *vagil baand;* the rope which tied the animal to the stake

# A plant of unbewitching (*Mòthan*)

In Uist the plant Mòthan, or Butterwort (*Pinguicula*) was believed to be a sure protection against the powers of witches. It should be pulled on a Sunday in this manner: - On finding a place where it grew in abundance, the person going to use it would mark out three small tufts, and calling one by the name of the Father, another by the name of the Son, and the third by the name of the Holy Ghost, would commence pulling the tufts, at the same time saying: -

*Buainidh mise am Mòthan,*
*An luibh a bheannaich an Domhnach;*
*Fhad 'sa ghleidheas mise am Mòthan*
*Cha 'n 'eil e beo air thalamh*
*Gin a bheir bainne mo bhò bhuam.*

**Translation:**

I will pull the *Mòthan*,
The herb blessed by the Domhnach;
So long as I preserve the *Mòthan*
Their lives not on earth,
One who will take my cow's milk from me.

The three tufts having thus been pulled, they were carefully taken home, rolled up in a small piece of cloth, and concealed in some comer of the dairy or milk-kist - '*ciste-a'-bhainne.*'

William Mackenzie. *Gaelic Incantations, Charms and Blessing of the Hebrides*

**130**

# Another Herb for unbewitching (*Torrannan*)

Buaineams' thu, a thorrannain,
Le t' uile bheannachd 's le t' uile bhuaidh ;
Thainig na naoi earrannan
Le buaidh an torrannain,
Lamh Bhrighde leam!
Tha mi nis 'gad bhuain.
Buaineams' thu, a thorrannain,
Le d' thoradh mara 's tire,
Ri lionadh gun traghadh
Le d' laimh-sa, Bhrighde mhin,
Calum naomh 'gam sheoladh,
Odhran caomh 'gam dhion,
Is Micheil nan steud uaibhreach
'Cur buaidh anns an ni.
Tha mo bis lurach a nis air a bhuain.

**Translation:**

Let me pluck thee, *Torannan*\*!
With all thy blessedness and all thy virtue,
The nine blessings came with the nine parts,
By the virtue of the *Torannan*;
The hand of St Bride with me, I am now to pluck thee.
Let me pluck thee, *Torannan*!
With thine increase as to sea and land;
With the flowing tide that shall know no ebbing,
By the assistance of the chaste St Bride,
The holy St Columba directing me,
Gentle Oran protecting me,
And St Michael of high-crested steeds
Imparting virtue to my cattle,
My darling plant is now plucked.

---

**Note:** *Torranann* is the Gaelic word for the plant known as Figwort (*Scrophularia*) and this charm must be spoken in the gathering of the herb.

## To Counteract a witch's spell or

## any other devilish charms

This magical formula was used by Isabel Pott, the wise woman of Cross, in Rockcliff who helped a said Francis Armestrang who had been bewitched. To perform it you must first burn on hot coals a mixer of sea salt and Rowan wood all the while it's performed. You must take three locks of the persons hair, three pieces of their shirt, three roots of wormwood, three of mugwort, three pieces of Rowan wood, and boil all together and anoint themselves with it and take three sips of the potion. The bewitched person was to keep their windows, doors and chimney shut, and the suspected person who is wronged will come to your door, but you must deny them access and then would their witchcraft and the devil's charms no longer be set on you.

A Mary Tate had gone to Isabel Pot in the Parish of Rockcliff, and declared that she ordered her that a South running water to be Lifted in the name of Father, Son, & Holy Ghost, and to be boiled at night in the house where Francis Armstrong was, with nettle roots, wormwood, mugwort, southernwood, and rowantree, and his hands, Legs, & temples be stroaked therewith, and three sups to be put in his mouth, and withal to keep the door close: She ordered also three locks of his hair to be burnt in the fire with three pieces dipt out of his shirt, and a Slut (rag dipt in tallow), to be lighted and carried round his bed, and all to be kept secret except from his near friends.

---

William George Black. *Charms and Spells at Gretna*

# Casting the *Caim*

The *Caim* or the "encompassing", is a form of safeguarding common in the west of Scotland. The encompassing of any of the Three Persons of the Trinity, the Blessed Virgin, the Apostles, or any of the saints may be invoked, according to the faith of the suppliant. In making the *Caim*, the suppliant stretches out the right hand with the forefinger extended and turns round sunwise (as if on a pivot), describing a circle with the tip of the forefinger while invoking the desired protection. The circle encloses the suppliant and accompanies him as he walks onward, safeguarded from all evil without or within. Protestant or Catholic, educated or illiterate, may make the ' caim ' in fear, danger, or distress, as when some untoward noise is heard, or some untoward object seen during the night:

*Aim Dhe agus a làmh dheas*
*Bhith dha m' chre agus dha m' chneas ;*
*Caim an Ardrigh 's gràs na Trianaid*
*Bhith orm a' tàmh an dàil na siorrachd,*
*Bhith orm a' tamh an dàil na siorrachd.*
*Caim nan Tri dha m' dhion am chuid,*
*Caim nan Tri dha m' dhion an diugh,*
*Caim nan Tri dha m' dhion a nochd*
*O ghoimh, o ghiamh, o ghniomh, o lochd,*
*O ghoimh, o ghiamh, o ghniomh, o lochd.*

**Translates:**

The compassing of God and His right hand
Be upon my form and upon my frame ;
The compassing of the High King and the grace of the Trinity
Be upon me abiding ever eternally,
Be upon me abiding ever eternally.
May the compassing of the Three shield me in my means,

The compassing of the Three shield me this day,
The compassing of the Three shield me this night
From hate, from harm, from act, from ill.
From hate, from harm, from act, from ill.

**Or**

*Aim Dhè bhith umad,*
*Caim Dhè nan dùla.*
*Caim Chrìosd bhith umad,*
*Caim Chrìosda chùmha.*
*Caim Spioraid umad,*
*Caim Spioraid Nùmha.*
*Caim nan Trì bhith umad,*
*Caim nan Trì dha d' chùmhna,*
*Caim nan Trì dha d' chùmhna.*

**Translates:**

The compassing of God be on thee,
The compassing of the God of He.
The compassing of Christ be on thee,
The compassing of the Christ of love.
The compassing of Spirit be on thee.
The compassing of the Spirit of Grace.
The compassing of the Three be on thee.
The compassing of the Three preserve thee.
The compassing of the Three preserve thee.

The Caim is my go-to when it comes when it comes to
precautions and protection against unknown harm, both for spiritual
and mundane purposes. There have been several spells recorded

**134**

when it comes to casting the Caim but I have mentioned here a few which I find both sufficient and effective.

For some, the casting of a circle or a compass-round is protocol for similar purposes, but in my practice, it is simply casting the Caim that is sufficient for me. As it is true to many other folk magic practitioners within Scotland. There has been many a time on my travels, going through a graveyard, woodlands, glen etc I have felt a presence around me or a feeling I my gut which has caused me concern for making the Caim. In Fact, whenever I walk the land with a spiritual conquest or working in mind, I make the Caim around myself for safe measure, just in case if there are any nasties about which means me harm. In making the Caim, I have always said to folks that although the Gaelic Christian "power of the Three" may be needed in this magical rite, it is the conjunction of three components of the action, visualization, and the charm spoken that makes the Caim so effective in the magical safeguarding.

---

Alexander Carmichael. *Carmina Gadelica, Vol. III*

## A Spell against all harm

*The charm Mary put around her son,*
*And [St] Bridget put on her banner,*
*And [St] Michael put on his shield,*
*And the son of God put before*
*His throne of clouds,*
*A charm thous art against sorrow,*
*A charm against sword,*
*A charm against red-tracked bullet,*
*An island thou art in sea,*
*A rock thou art on land,*

*And greater be the fear those have,*
*Of the body round which charm goes,*
*In the presence of Colum-kill (St. Columba),*
*With his mantle (Cloak) around thee.*

---

Michael Howard. *Scottish Witches and Warlocks*

## To be shot-free in war

This charm was said to be taught on to pope Leo from the angels to protect oneself from being shot in war, which the four Evangelists, and the crosses between them on a piece of virgin parchment or paper, and carried about you:

*Jesus + Chrisus + Messias + Sotar + Emmanuel*

---

George Sinclair. *Satan's invisible world discovered*

## The House protecting charm.

### (*teisreadh taighe*)

| | |
|---|---|
| *Dhe, beannaich an ce 's na bheil ann,* | God, bless the world and all that is therein. |
| *Dhe, beannaich mo cheile is mo chlann,* | God, bless my spouse and my children, |
| *Dhe, beannaich an re a ta 'na m' cheann,* | God, bless the eye that is in my head, |
| *Is beannaich, a Dhe, laimhseachadh mo laimh;* | And bless, O God, the handling of my hand; |
| *An am domh eirigh 's a mhaduinn mhoich,* | What time I rise in the morning early, |
| *Is laighe air leabaidh anamoich,* | What time I lie down late in bed, |

136

*Beannaich m' eirigh 's a*
*mhaduinn mhoich,*
*Is mo laighe air leabaidh*
*anamoich.*

*Dhe, teasruig an teach 's an t-*
*ardrach,*
*Dhe, coistrig a chlann mhathrach,*
*Dhe, cuartaich an spreidh 's an t-*
*alach;*
*Bi-sa fein na'n deigh 's da'n taladh,*
*Duair dhireas ni ri frith 's ri fruan,*
*Duair shineas mi a sios an suan,*
*Duair dhireas ni ri frith 's ri*
*fruan,*
*Duair shineas mi an sith gu*
*suan.*

Bless my rising in the morning
early,
And my lying down late in bed.

God, protect the house, and the
household,
God, consecrate the children of the
motherhood,
God, encompass the flocks and the
young;
Be Thou after them and tending
them,
What time the flocks ascend hill and
wold,
What time I lie down to sleep,
What time the flocks ascend hill
and wold,
What time I lie down in peace to
sleep

---

Alexander Carmichael. *Carmina Gadelica, Vol I*

## Blessing of the House

## *(Beannachadh Taighe)*

*Dhe, beannaich an taigh,*
*Bho steidh gu staidh,*
*Bho chrann gu fraigh,*
*Bho cheann gu saidh,*
*Bho dhronn gu traigh,*
*Bho sgonn gu sgaith,*

*Eadar bhonn agus bhraighe,*
*Bhonn agus bhraighe.*

**Translates:**

God bless the house,
From site to stay,
From beam to wall,
From end to end,
From ridge to basement,
From balk to roof-tree,
From found to summit,
Found and summit.

---

Alexander Carmichael. *Carmina Gadelica, Vol I*

# Saining, Hollowing and Blessings

## The Washing-charm for New-borns

When washing new-born babies, wise women made use of this charm to bless the wee bairn:

*Hale fair washing to thee,*
*Hale washing of the Fíans be thine,*
*Heath to thee, heath to him,*
*But not to thy female enemy.*

---

John Gregerson campbell. *Witchcraft and the second sight in the Highlands & Islands of Scotland*

# The Bathing Charm

## (*eolas an fhailcidh*)

The water having been duly blessed, the woman bathing the infant began by sprinkling a palmful (*boiseag*) of water on its head. As the charm went on, and as each palmful was sprinkled on the child, the following Incantation was repeated:

*Boiseagorr h-aois [air t-aois],*
*'S boiseag orr fhas [air t-fhas],*
*A's air do chuid a ghabhail ort,*
*'S a chuid nach fhasadh anns an oidhche dhiot*
*Gu'm fasadh anns an latha dhiot.*
*Tri baslaichean na Trianaid Naoimh,*
*Ga d' dhion 's ga d' shabhaladh*
*Bho bheum sial,*
*'S bho chraos-fharmad nam peacach.*

### Translates:
A palmfull of water on your age [years],
A palmfull of water on your growth.
And on your taking of your food;
And may the part of you which grows not during
the night
Grow during the day.
Three palmfuls of water of the Holy Trinity,
To protect and guard you
From the effects of the evil eye.
And from the jealous lust of sinners.

---

William Mackenzie; '*Gaelic Incantations, Charms and Blessing of the Hebrides*'.

# A Spell for making Butter come.

When butter wont churn, this charm must be said over it:

*Come butter, come,*

*Come butter, come:*

*Peter stands at the gate,*

*Waiting for a butter'd cake,*

*Come butter, come!*

---

Thomas Davidson. *Rowan tree and Red Thread*

## The *Seun, Sian* or Sain

The seun or sian, in Scots; Sain, was used for the protection of both man and beast from dangers, such as being taken away by an enemy, being drowned, or struck by sword, or arrow, or bullet in battle. It consisted of rhymes, or parti-coloured strings, or plants, and in many cases its nature remained a mystery. It was said over cows and sheep when leaving them for the night; it was put round the necks of infants; given by the fairy mistress (*leannan sìth*) to her earthly lover; sewn by the foster-mother (*muime*) in the clothes of a beloved foster-son (dalta) about to leave her, etc. After it was once given or said, the two, the giver and the recipient, must not see each other again. If they did the charm lost its power. Usually there was some unforeseen danger of the class which the charm was intended to provide against that proved fatal. Thus, it is said, a young woman gave a *sian* to her soldier lover, who was leaving for foreign wars, telling him the only thing he had to guard against was his own arms. He went scatheless through a protracted war, but after his return scratched his forehead with a pin which he carried in his clothes and died from the effects.

---

# The Sain

## (*sian*)

There was no action recorded, or what exactly this spell was used for, but I have used this spell many saining rites in general and crossing myself and/or the object after it has been recited:

| | |
|---|---|
| *Sian a chuir Moir air a Mac,* | The sain put by Mary on her Son, |
| *Sian romh mharbhadh,* | Sain from death, sain from wound, |
| *sian romh lot,* | |
| *Sian eadar cioch agus glun,* | Sain from breast to knee, |
| *Sian eadar glun agus lorc,* | Sain from knee to foot, |
| *Sian nan tri sian,* | Sain of the three sains, |
| *Sian nan coig sian,* | Sain of the five sains, |
| *Sian nan seachd sian,* | Sain of the seven sains, |
| *Eadar barr do chinn* | From the crown of thy head |
| *Agus bonn do chos.* | To the soles of thy feet. |
| *Sian nan seachd paidir, a h-aon,* | Sain of the seven paters, one, |
| *Sian nan seachd paidir, a dha,* | Sain of the seven paters, two, |
| *Sian nan seachd paidir, a tri,* | Sain of the seven paters, three, |
| *Sian nan seachd paidir, a ceithir,* | Sain of the seven paters, four, |
| *Sian nan seachd paidir, a coig,* | Sain of the seven paters, five, |
| *Sian nan seachd paidir, a sia,* | Sain of the seven paters, six, |
| *Sian nan seachd paidir, a seachd* | Sain of the seven paters, seven |
| *Ort a nis.* | Upon thee now. |
| | From the edge of thy brow, |
| | To thy coloured soles, |
| | To preserve thee from behind, |

**141**

*Bho chlaban do bhathas,*
*Gu dathas do bhonn,*
*Ga d' chumail o d' chul,*
*Ga d' chumhn o t'*
*aghaidh.*

*Clogad slainne mu d'*
*cheann,*
*Cearcul comhnant mu d'*
*bhraigh,*
*Uchd-eididh an t-sagairt mu*
*d' bhrollach,*
*Ga d' dhion an cogadh 's an*
*comhrag nan namh.*

*Ma's ruaig dhuit, oig, o*
*thaobh do chuil,*
*Buaidh na h-Oigh ga do*
*chomhnadh dluth,*
*Sear no siar, siar no sear,*
*Tuath no deas, deas no tuath.*

To sustain thee in front.

Be the helmet of salvation about
thine head,
Be the corslet of the covenant about
thy throat,
Be the breastplate of the priest upon
thy breast,
To shield thee in the battle and
combat of thine enemies.

If pursued, oh youth, from
behind thy back,
The power of the Virgin be close to
succour thee,
East or west, west, or east,
North or south, south or north.

Alexander Carmichael. *Carmina Gadelica, Vol II*

## To *sain* or protection the house at night

*Who sains the house the night,*
*They that sains it ilka night,*
*Saint Bríde and her bràt,*
*Saint colme (Columba) and his hat,*
*Saint Michael and his spear,*
*Keep this house from the weir;*
*From running thief,*
*And burning thief,*

*And from and ill Rea,*
*That be the gate can gae,*
*And from ane ill weight (wright),*
*That be the gate can light,*
*Nine reeds about the house,*
*Keep it all the night,*
*What is that, what I see?*
*So red, So bright, beyond I see!*
*'tis he was pierc'd through the hands,*
*Through the feet, through the throat,*
*Through the tongue;*
*Through the liver and the lung.*
*Well is them that well may*
*Fast on good Friday.*

Although this charm can be use anytime to sain the house, I also take the opportunity to give my home a good saining on Good Friday and the feast days of the saints mentioned in this spell:

St. Bride's day - *1ˢᵗ February*
St. Colm (Columba) day- *9ᵗʰ June*
St. Michael's day- *29ᵗʰ September*
Good Friday- *the Friday before Easter Sunday*

---

George Sinclair. *Satan's invisible world discovered*

## The Three lairds land cure

A yard of yarn must be held together from end to end, making a circlet which the patient must pass through it three times for their illness to be transmitted, and cut into nine parts and buried in "three lord's lands". Another alternative which is used for both divination and cures, was to wash a patient's clothing in a river where "three laird's lands meet" and all the while performing the operation in silence. In fact, some ladies would refuse to speak before passing the boundary of her land, and there sat down and plaiting (braiding) her hair betwixt the marker stones.

**143**

## Ninth Wave water

The magical qualities of ninth wave water was first mentioned in The Book of Invasions *(Lebor Gabála Érenn)* In the tales the coming of the sons of Mill, where after truce, the Tuatha Dé Danann tricked the Milesians by forcing them to withdraw back to sea and drop anchor beyond the ninth wave. After this they was unable to set sail by to land and allowed the Tuatha Dé Danann to use magic to brew up a storm and send it towards the Milesian ships. It seems in this case the Ninth water was used for shielding and protection against the invaders. In many parts of the world, local folklore predicts that out of a certain number of waves, one will be much larger than the rest. "Every seventh wave" or "every ninth wave" are examples of such common beliefs that have wide circulation.

Water taken from the tops of three waves was in Shetland believed to cure toothache.

George. F Black. *Orkney and Shetland Islands*

## Forespoken Water

Forespoken water is water which something has been dropped into, supposed to possess magical powers, and over which an Incantation has been pronounced, - probably a reminiscence of Holy Water. The articles dropped in the water were, as a rule, three pebbles of different colours gathered from the seashore. The charm was considered most potent when one stone was jet black, another white, and the remaining red, blue, or greenish.

An incantation was then muttered over the water, the reciter commencing by saying the word "Sain," and at the same time making the sign of the cross on the surface of the water. The incantation was as follows:

> *In the name of Him that can cure or kill,*
> *This water shall cure all earthy ill,*
> *Shall cure the blood and flesh and bone,*
> *For ilka ane there is a stone;*
> *May she fleg all trouble, sickness, pain.*
> *Cure without and cure within.*
> *Cure the heart, and horn, and skin.*

The patient for whom the " Forespoken Water " was prepared had to drink a part of it; the remainder was sprinkled on his person.

When the Beasts as Oxen, Sheep, Horses, &c., are Sick, they sprinkle them with a Water made up by them, which they call Forespoken Water \ wherewith like ways they sprinkle their Boats, when they succeed and prosper not in their Fishing. And especially on Hallow-Even, they use to sein or sign their Boats and put a Cross of Tar upon them, which my Informer hath often seen. Their Houses also some use then to *sein* or sain.

---

George. F Black. *Orkney and Shetland Islands*

## The Keppoch Charm

There was a charm stone which was owned by the Macdonnells of Keppoch which was used to cure several illnesses. The charm is "an oval of rock-crystal, about the size of a small egg, fixed in a bird's claw of silver, and with a silver chain attached, by which it was suspended when about to be dipped." While the charm was dipped in water gathered from the holy well, this incantation was said:

> *Bogam thu 'sa bhùrn,*
> *A lèug bhuidhe, bhoidheach, bhuadhar.*
> *Ann am bùrn an fhior-uisg;*

*Nach d' leig Bride a thruailleadh,*

*An ainm nan Abstol naomh,*
*S Muire Oigh nam beùsan,*

*'N ainm na Trianaid ard,*
*'S nan aingeal dealrach uile;*
*Beannachd air an lèug;*
*'S beannachd air an uisge,*
*Leigheas tinneas clèibh do gach creutair*
*cuirte*

**Translates:**

Let me dip thee in the water,
Thou yellow, beautiful gem of
Power!
In water of purest wave,
Which (Saint) Bridget didn't
permit to be contaminated.
In the name of the Apostles
twelve,
In the name of Mary, Virgin of
virtues,

And in the name of the High
Trinity
And all the shining angels,
A blessing on the gem,
A blessing on the water, and
A healing of bodily ailments to
each suffering creature..

The reference to St Bridget in the incantation, it is necessary to
mention that there is a well near Keppoch, called *Tobar-Bhride*

(Bridget's Well), from which a small stream runs from it. It was from this stream that the water was taken into which the charm-stone was to be dipped. There was no mention in how the water in which it was dipped was administered to the patient, but my professional guess would to be drunk or sprinkled over the patient as is quite popular in Scottish folk magic. I have a similar bird's claw pendent which I use to make *sained* or blessed water, but I don't see why any stone used by the practitioner could be used incorporation of the magical action and incantation.

F. Marian McNeill. *The Silver Bough vol. I*
Electric Scotland. *Scottish Charms and Amulets* [online source]

# Cures, Healing and Charming

## The Three-knot charm
### *(An Snairm)*

The *Snairm* (Three-knot charm) was used by people of the healing art or had the *Eolas* (knowledge) for all manner of illness and unbewitching.

She then caused everyone to leave the room where the sick lad was, and getting a ball of red yarn, three ply, she wound it round the points of her thumb, mid-finger, and ring-finger of her left hand, taking care to hold the thread while winding it between the thumb and mid-finger of her right hand.

Having wound it in this manner, she took a small piece of burning stick and passed it three times through the circle formed by the thread, which remained as it had been wound on the fingers of her left hand. She then put a knot on the thread, and while doing so brought it near her lips, at the same time going through a lengthy incantation, beginning with the words " *Ni mi an obair so*" (I do this work), and in which there were frequent allusions to the eye. When the knot had been put on and the charm had been repeated, she took the yarn off her fingers, and, commencing at the crown of the lad's head, she rubbed him in a round and round way all over. At this stage a knock " came to the door," and the performer called out, "You are there, I know you." Without opening the door, she put the knotted yarn into the fire, saying, "*An galar's easlainnte chuirinn air mulach an teine* " (I put the disease and the sickness on the top of the fire). This she repeated three times, but on the third occasion, instead of putting the thread on the fire, she tied it round the lad's neck. He got well at once. The thread is always tied somewhere that it may not be seen, but it must be on the skin. The woman explained that the knock at the door while she was performing the cure was the act of the one who had done the injury. Another woman who had the "*Eolas*" proceeded to wind the yarn round her fingers as described above, and it is explained that the [online source]

forefinger must not be allowed to touch the 'yarn during the performance of the charm. She then took what she had wound off her fingers, opened it, and put a knot on the thread, which she held to her lips, muttering the charm.

Although the lengthy incantation is not given, there is many charms to pick from in this book. The smoking stick used for passing through the loop of threads is not mentioned, Juniper, cedar or Rowan is used within Scottish folk magic for saining, curing and protection.

R. C. Maclagan. *Notes on Folklore Objects Collected in Argyleshire*

# The Triple Threads

## (*eolas an t-snaithnean*)

I have previously pointed out that Pennant, in his Tour, refers to VirgiFs description of the charms used by the shepherd Alphesiboeus, and the use of triple threads in connection with these:

*"Necte triims nodis ternosy Amarylli, colores ;*

*Necte, Amarylli, modo et ' Veneris' dic * vinctda ne*


("Twine in three knots, Amaryllis, the three colours;

Twine them, Amaryllis, and say, 'I am twining the bonds of love".)


*Eolas an t-Snaithnean* is simply the Charm or Incantation of the threads, that is, the triple threads; and it is worthy of note that the triple threads of Virgil were white, rose colour, and black. In Virgil's Ecologue VIII., line 73, we have a clear reference to the *Eolas* of the triple threads:


*"Tema tibi hxec primum triplici diversa colore*

*Licia circumdo,"*

("These three threads distinct with three colours

I wind round thee tìrst ")


Thus, proving the great antiquity of this charm. It is still very popular in the Western Islands and is used as a Charm against the effects of the Evil Eye, and against Witchcraft. The rite observed is as follows:

—

First, the *Paidir* or Pater is said. Then the following Incantation:

*Chi suil thu,*

*Labhraidh bial thu;*

*Smuainichidh cridhe thu.*

*Tha Fear an righthighe*

*Gad' choisreagadh,*

*An t-Athair, am Mac, 's an Spiorad Naomh.*


*Ceathrar a rinn do chron*

*Fear agus bean,*

*Gille agus nighean.*

*Co tha gu sin a thiueadh ì*

*Tri Pearsannan na Trianaid ro-naomh,*

*An t-Athair, ani Mac, 's an Spiorad Naomh.*


*Tha mi 'cur fianuis gu Moire, agus gu Brighde,*

*Ma 's e duine rinn do chron,*

*Le droch run,*

*No le droch shuil,*

*No le droch chridhe,*

*Gu'm bi thusa, gu math*

*Ri linn so a chur mu 'n cuairt ort.*

*An ainm an Athar, a' Mhic, 's an Spioraid Naoimh.*

**Translates:**

An eye will see you,

Tongue will speak of you,

Heart will think of you,

The Man of Heaven

Blesses you

The Father, Son, and Holy Ghost.

Four caused your hurt —

Man and wife,

Young man and maiden.

Who is to frustrate that?

The three Persons of the most Holy Trinity,

The Father, Son, and Holy Ghost.


I call the Virgin Mary and St Bridget to witness

That if your hurt was caused by man,

Through ill-will,

Or the evil eye,

Or a wicked heart,

That you [name] may be whole,

While I entwine this about you.

The whole of the foregoing Incantation is recited three times, and, during the recital, the *Snaithnean*, or tri-coloured triple thread, is entwined about the beast's tail (*am Imn an earhuill*) with triple knots. If the beast is to recover, the person applying the *Snaithnean* feels himself or herself becoming ill. If the first recital does not prove efficacious, the rite may be performed two or three times.

William Mackenzie. *Gaelic Incantations, Charms and Blessing of the Hebrides*

## Casting the Heart.

It was formerly believed that when an individual was attenuated by sickness, his heart was worn away or taken from him by some evil genii. A person skilled in casting the heart was at once sent for, who, with many mysterious ceremonies, melted lead and poured it through the bowl of a key or pair of scissors held over a sieve, which was also placed on a basin of cold water. The lead was melted and poured again and again till it assumed something like the form of a heart at least the operator strove to persuade his patients and his friends that such was the case. This was hung suspended from the neck till the cure was completed.

### *Another Method:*

The primary materials of the charm were lead and water. The lead was placed on the fire in a small pot or crucible, without handle. It seemed to be a needful part of the charm that the human hand should not touch the crucible, which was taken off the fire and carried to the water in the grip of a small pair of ordinary fire-tongs. The vessel containing the water must not touch the ground. It was placed on a small wooden frame, but not in contact therewith. Over the top of this wooden frame a pair of scissors and a horn comb were crossed, and over this cross of metal and organic substance was placed a small tub or '*luggie*', containing the water. Now came the crisis. The crucible of molten lead, held in the grip of the tongs, was poured from some height into the water, in which the falling stream of molten metal solidified in a great variety of curious shapes. These variously shaped pieces of lead were all carefully passed in review, and if one of them was a well-shaped heart, then the patient's heart was all right, and there was no need to go further with the charm. But if there was no well-formed heart, or nothing like a heart, then the whole of the lead was returned to the crucible, to be again, and if need be, many times, operated upon in the same way. If something resembling a heart were found, the process was repeated, in the belief that further approaches to a well-shaped heart in the metal would be accompanied by similarly ameliorative progress towards the patient's recovery. But if, after many trials, no well-shaped heart was found in the water, then the friends of the sufferer must prepare for the worst.

Ellen Emma Guthrie. *Old Scottish Customs: Local and General*

Donald Masson. *Notes from the North Highlands*

## Cures for Warts

A wart is removed by rubbing on it some earth from the sole of the foot when the new moon is first noticed, which will cause it to disappear before next new moon. A straw cut short, but preserving the knot, wetted in the mouth, and rubbed on the wart, then hid away where no eye can see it, causes the wart to disappear just as it rots in its secret place. The most effective way to remove a wart is to contrive all unknown to rub it against some article of apparel belonging to an adulterous person.

Another other way so of curing warts was putting in a bag as many knots or joints of straw or grass as there were warts to be banished and leaving them on the public road. The first person who lifted the bag got the warts in the future.

Pig's blood could also be applied to the warts and rubbed off with a cloth, which was then left on a road. The warts were transferred to the first person to pick up the cloth.

Cathel Kerr. *Fishermen and Superstition*

John Gregorson Campbell; Ed. Ronald Black. *The Gaelic otherworld'.*

## A Charm for cramp

Stand firmly on the leg affected, and repeat the appropriate gesture whilst chanting:

*The devil is tying a knot in my leg,*
*Matthew, Mark, Luke, and John, unloose it, I beg;*
*Crosses three we make to ease us,*
*Two for the thieves, and one for Jesus.*

Alexander MacBain. *Incantations and Magic Rhymes*

## A Scot's blood-staunching charm

*In the blud of Adam death was taken,*
*In the blud of Christ it was all slaken,*
*And by the same blud I do charge,*
*That thou do run nae longer at large.*

Michael Howard. *Scottish Witches and Warlocks*

# A blood stopping charm

This charm was used by the Gaels of the western isles and was said to have been used by Finn MacCool himself:

*Listen, O blood,*
*instead of flowing,*
*instead of pouring forth thy warm stream.*
*Stop, O blood, like a wall;*
*stop, like a hedge;*
*stop, like a reef in the sea;*
*like a stiff sedge in the moss;*
*like a boulder in a field;*
*like the pine in the wood.'*

---

Alexander MacBain. *Incantations and Magic Rhymes*


# The Wresting Thread

When a person has received a sprain, it is customary to apply to an individual practised in casting the 'wresting thread.' This is a thread spun from black wool, on which are cast nine knots, and tied round a sprained leg or arm. During the time the operator is putting the thread round the affected limb, he says, but in such a tone of voice as not to be heard by the bystanders, nor even by the person operated upon:

*The Lord rade,*
*And the foal slade;*
*He lighted.*
*And he righted.*
*Set joint to joint.*
*Bone to bone,*
*And sinew to sinew.*
*Heal in the Holy Ghost's name!*

In Orkney, a thread, having on it nine knots, was tied round the sprained part. As the thread was being tied the following Incantation was muttered:

*Nine knots upo' this thread.*
*Nine blessings on thy head;*
*Blessings to take away thy pain*
*And ilka tinter of thy strain.*

George. F Black. *Orkney and Shetland Islands*

## A Gaelic charm for healing a sprain.

The charmer must tie a "worsted thread" (Black thread) on the injured limb, whilst chanting this Gaelic charm:

*'Chaidh Criosd a mach*
*'S a' mhaduinn mhoich,*
*'S fhuiar e casan nan each,*
*Air am bristeadh mu seach.*
*Chuir e cnaimh ri cnaimh,*
*Agus feith ri feith,*
*Agus feoil ri feoil,*
*Agus craicionn ri craicionn,*
*'S mar leighis esan sin*
*Gu'n leighis mise so.'*

**Translation:**

Christ went out,
In the early morning,
And he found the feet of the horses,
Broken in turn.
He put bone to bone,
And vein to vein,
And flesh to flesh,
And skin to Skin,
And as he healed that,
May I heal this.

Alexander MacBain. *Incantations and Magic Rhymes*

## An Orkney charm Wormy Lines

Toothache in Sanday (Orkney) is called The Worm from a notion the country people have that this painful affection is caused by a worm in the tooth or jawbone. For the cure of this disease the following charm, called Wormy Lines, is written on a slip of paper, which must be sewed into some part of the dress of the person affected, and must be carried about with him as long as the paper lasts:

> *" Peter sat on a marble stone weeping,*
> *Christ came past and said, ' What aileth thee, Peter? '*
> *' O my Lord, my God, my tooth doth ache! '*
> *' Arise, O Peter, go thy way, thy tooth shall ache no more! '*

George. F Black. *Orkney and Shetland Islands*

## A Shetland charm for toothache

Traditionally, the earliest witches in the islands (Shetland and Orkney) were known to be 'Finns', and the author suggests that they possibly were aboriginal inhabitants of Norway who came over with the Scandinavian settlers. This said charm mentions in it these 'Finnmen;' as follows:

> *T'ree Finnnmen cam' fae heem I' de sea*
> *Fae de weary de folk for tae free,*
> *An' dey sall be paid wi' de white monie.*
> *Oot o' de flesh an' oot o' de bane;*
> *Oot o' de sinew, an oot o' de skin;*
> *Oot o' de skin an' om tae de stane.*
> *An' dere may du remain!*

*An 'dere may du remain!*
*An' dere may du remain!*


Although there is no mention of any action taken whilst reciting this incantation, the end of the second verse suggests the use of a stone. Perhaps finding a white stone on a beach and rubbing it on the affected area as is the popular action of charming in Scotland

A dead man's finger or a coffin nail would be put in the mouth of the sufferer, according to accounts, with those in pain ideally retrieving these items from the graveyard. However, it is believed this aspect of the charm was rarely carried out.

---

Earnest W. Marwick. *The Folklore of Orkney and Shetland'*.

John Gregorson Campbell; Ed. Ronald Black. *The Gaelic otherworld'*.

## To cure Ringworm
The person afflicted, with ringworm takes a few ashes, held between the forefinger and thumb, three successive mornings before tasting food, and, applying the ashes to the part afflicted, says -
*'Ringworm! ringworm red!*
*Never mayest thou either speed or spread;*
*But aye grow less and less,*
*And die away among the ase (ashes).'*
*At the same time, he throws the ashes, held between the finger and thumb,*
*into the fire.*

---

Ellen Emma Guthrie. *Old Scottish Customs: Local and General*

# To Cure Fever

*Painful fever, violent fever,*
*The fever which never leaves man,*
*Unremitting fever,*
*The lingering fever, malignant fever,*
*Spirit of the heavens, cunjure it!*
*Spirit of the Earth, cunjure it!*

Alexander MacBain. *Incantations and Magic Rhymes*

# For Affections of the Chest.

*I will trample on thee, tightness,*
*As on mountain dust to-night;*
*On thyself be thy blackening, dwarfing power*
*Evil and painful is that.*
*The charm which Patrick put*
*On the mother of the son of the King of Iver,*
*To kill the worms*
*Round the veins of her heart,*
*For the four and twenty afflictions*
*In her constitution;*
*For the water of the running stream of her boundary,*
*For the stones of the earth's waves,*
*For the weakness of her heart,*
*For jaundice and distemper,*
*For withering and for asthma.*

John Gregorson Campbell. *Witchcraft & second sight in the Highlands & Islands*

# To cure a stye the eye
## (*leamhnuid*)

He is to repeat the following without once drawing breath:

*Thainig Cailleach a Loch Abair*
*'Shireadh scadain a Loch Bhraoin,*
*Cha d'iarr i air peighinn*
*Ach 'n a chunntadh i gun anail,*
*Scidear scadan aon, scidear, scadan dha, scidear scadan tri . . . . scidear*
*scadan ceud.*

**Translation:**
Cailleach came to Lochaber,
Herring to Loch Broom,
She didn't ask him to pay
But when she was counting without beath,

Herrring skidder one, Skidder, herring two, herring skidder three.
. . . a hundred herring skidders

Should this charm be said as requested, it was supposed to be very effective. One end of a stick was in the fire until it burned and then pointed at the poor eye. It would then be quickly moved around in a circle while reciting "*A stye one, a stye two, a stye three....*" The charm would be said up to the number nine with the line added "*take yourself off, stye*". Some would rub the stye with a piece of gold.

---

Cathel Kerr. *Fishermen and Superstition*

John Gregorson Campbell; Ed. Ronald Black. *The Gaelic otherworld'.*

# To recover someone from a fit or seizer

When the patient is in the fit, if someone puts his mouth over the ear of the patient, and says three times those three verses: -

*Gaspar fert mirrham thus Melchior Bathasar aurum*
*Haec tria, qui secum porlabit nomina regum,*
*Solvitur à morbo Christi pietate caduco.*

**Translation:**
Gaspar carries myrrh thus Melchior gold
Balthasar [Frankincense]
These three elements, the names of the kinds who
were with him portrait,
In front of a mortal disease devoted to Christ.

Without doubt he will get up at once. That this is efficacious when repeated in the ear is true, and it has often been proved, that he gets up at once. And it is said that the same verses written and worn round the neck cure entirely.

---

Dr. A. Clerk. *Notes on Ancient Gaelic Medicine*

# John Dougall's cure for convulsion fits

## (1695)

The prescribed as a cure for convulsion fits, the paring of the sick man's nails, the pulling of his eyebrows, and some hairs from the crown of his head, which nail-pairings and hair clippings were 'to be bound up in a clout with a halfpenny, and laid down on such a place, and that whoever found this would take the disease, and the diseased be set free.

## Dougall's charm for "sturdie".

Take 'the cutting off a stirk's head, boiling it, burning the bones to ashes, and burying the ashes,' a remedy which, as Dougall stoutly maintained before the Presbytery, was 'most effectual.

Alex Gardner. *A History of The Witches of Renfrewshire*

## To cure a Burn

To cure a burn, the following words were used:

> *'Here come I to cure a burnt sore;*
> *If the dead knew what the living endure*
> *The burnt sore would burn no more.'*

The operator, after having repeated the above, blows his breath three times upon the burnt place. The above recipe was believed to have been communicated to a daughter who had been burned by the spirit of her deceased mother.

Ellen Emma Guthrie. *Old Scottish Customs: Local and General*

## An Orkney charm for telling out the *Swey*

The pain occasioned by a burn or scald is here [in Sanday] called *Swey* or *Sweying*. To relieve the *Swey* this charm is employed, and must be repeated by a wise one in private:

> *A dead wife out of the grave arose,*
> *And through the Sea she swimmed;*
> *Through the Water made to the cradle;*
> *God save the Bairn burnt sair!*
> *Het fire, cool soon in God's name!*

Another to cure a burn, the following words are used:

> *Here come I to cure a burnt sore;*
> *If the dead knew what the living endure,*
> *The burnt sore would burn no more.*

The operator, after having repeated the above, blows his breath three times upon the burnt place. The above is recorded to have been communicated to a daughter who had been burned, by the spirit of her deceased mother.

George. F Black. *Orkney and Shetland Islands*

## A Shetland charm for ringworm

The person afflicted with ringworm takes a little ash between the forefinger and thumb, three successive mornings, and before havng taken any food and holding the ashes to the part affected, says:

*Ringworm! ringworm red!*
*Never mayest thou either spread or speed;*
*But aye grow less and less,*
*And die away among the ase.*

At the same time, throwing the little ashes held between the forefinger and thumb into the fire.

George. F Black. *Orkney and Shetland Islands*

## An Orkney charm for Stemming blood.

For suppressing haemorrhage, as spitting of blood, bleeding from the nose, bleeding from a wound, &c., the following charm is solemnly repeated once, twice, or oftener, according to the urgency of the case, by some old man or woman accounted more sagacious than their neighbours. It is not to be repeated aloud, nor in the presence of any one but the patient:

*Three Virgins came across Jordan Sand,*
*Each with a bloody knife in her hand;*
*Stem blood, stem! tetherly stand!*
*Bloody Nose (or Mouth, &c.) in God's name mend!*

They have a Charm, whereby they stop excessive blooding in any, whatever way they come by it, whether by or without External Violence. The name of the Patient being sent to the Charmer, he saith over some words (which I heard) upon which the Blood instantly stopped, though the blooding Patient were at the greatest distance from the Charmer. Yea upon the saying of these words, the Blood will stop in the blooding Throats of Oxen or Sheep, to the astonishment of Spectators."

George. F Black. *Orkney and Shetland Islands*

## Some bizarre formulas to cure poor mental health.

It was said the following cure should only be tried on a Thursday. A person took the sufferer behind him on a grey horse and gallop at the horse's fastest pace three times round a boundary mark before riding to an immovable stone. Here, the sufferer would be forced to speak to the stone - with the cure then said to be complete.

In the Hebrides, it is said the sufferer would be tied with a rope around the waist and then attached to a boat and pulled 'till he was nearly dead'.

Disclaimer: I certainly wouldn't recommend anyone perform the actions in these formulas as an attempt to "cure" yourself of poor mental health and have only included it in this book for historical value.

John Gregorson Campbell; Ed. Ronald Black. *The Gaelic otherworld'.*

# Miscellaneous

## For Plaiting thread for magic

I chant this verse which I have adapted and taken from one of Walter Scott's poems in a form of an incantation which I call the *twist ye, twine ye charm* and use when plaiting (braiding) threads or cord of three, four or six for:

> *"Twist ye, twine ye! Even so,*
> *Mingle threads of joy and woe,*
> *Hope and fear and peace and strife,*
> *Tis the threads of human life"*

Sir Walter Scott. *Twist ye, Twine ye* (1890)

## The Nine-knotted clew or cord charm

Although this chant was originally used a charm for bewitchment, I have used when tying the nine knotted clew or when creating the Wresting threads:

> *"Da twal, da twal Apostles;*
> *Da 'leven, da 'leven Evangelists;*
> *Da ten, da ten Commandments;*
> *Da nine, da brazen shiners;*
> *Da eight, da holy waters;*
> *Da seven, da stars o' heaven;*
> *Da six, Creation's dawnin;*
> *Da five, da timblers o' da bools;*
> *Da four, da gospel makers;*
> *Da tree, da triddle treevers;*
> *Da twa lily white boys that clothe themselves*
> *In green;*

*Da een, da een dat walks alon', an' evermore*
*Sall rue"*

The modern incantation used for trying the nine knotted cord charm may as well have been inspired by the chant above, as follows with both the application and chant:

By the knot of one, the spell's begun

1------------------------------------------------------------------------

By knot of two, it cometh true

x-----------------------------------------------------------------------2

by the knot of three, thus it shall be

x-----------------------------3-----------------------------------------x

By the knot of four, it's strengthened more

x----------------4-----------------x----------------------------------x

By the knot of Five, the spell shall thrive

x---------------x---------------x------------------5------------------x

By the knot of Six, this spell I fix

X-----------6-------------x-------------x--------------x------------x

By the knot of seven, the stars of heaven

x----------x---------- -x--------- 7----------x---------x-----------x

By the knot of eight, the hand of fate

x---------x---------x--------x--------x-------8-------x--------x

By the knot of nine, what's done is mine

x-------x--------x-------x-------x--------x-------x--------9-------x

## A thief's charm for stealing goods.

This charm was used in the Scottish borders by thieves and robbers wishing to steal meat and not get caught:

*He that ordin'd us to be born,*

*Send us more [meat] for the morn,*

*Part of't right and part of't wrang,*

*God let us never fast owre lang,*

*God be thanked, and our Lady,*

*All is done that we have ready.*

---

George Sinclair. *Satan's invisible world discovered*

## Prayer for Travelling.

### (*ora turais*)

This hymn was sung by a pilgrim in setting out on his pilgrimage. The family and friends joined the traveller in singing the hymn and starting the journey, from which too frequently, for various causes, he never returned

*BITH a bhi na m' bhial,*
*Bladh a bhi na m' chainn,*
*Blath na siri na mo bhile,*
*Gun an tig mi nail.*

LIFE be in my speech,
Sense in what I say,
The bloom of cherries on my lips,
Till I come back again.

*An gaol thug Iosa Criosda*

The love Christ Jesus gave

*Bhi lionadh gach cridhe domh,*
*An gaol thug Iosa Criosda*
*Da m' lionadh air an son.*

Be filling every heart for me,
The love Christ Jesus gave
Filling me for every one.

*Siubhal choire, siubhal choille,*
*Siubhal fraoine fada, fas,*
*Moire mhin-gheal sior dha m'*
*chobhair,*
*Am Buachaill Iosa m' dhion 's a*
*char.*
*Moire mhin-gheal sior dha m'*
*chobhair,*
*Am Buachaill Iosa m' dhion 's a*
*chas.*

Traversing corries, traversing
forests,
Traversing valleys long and wild.
The fair white Mary still uphold
me,
The Shepherd Jesu be my shield,
The fair white Mary still uphold
me,
The Shepherd Jesu be my shield.

---

Alexander Carmichael. *Carmina Gadelica, Vol I*

## Big Allan's charm for winning in court.

Whenever Big Allan of Woodend (*Ailein Mór Cheannacoille*), in Kingairloch was pulled up by the law for abusive language, when entering the courthouse, he would spit in his fist, grasp his staff firmly, and say these following words:

*I will close my fist,*
*Faithful to me is the wood;*
*It is to protect my abusive words*
*I enter in,*
*The three sons of Clooney will save me*
*And Manaman MacLeth,*
*And St. Columba, gentle cleric,*
*And Alexander in Heaven!*

---

John Gregerson Campbell. *Witchcraft and the second*

# The *Fath-fith*

The *Fàth-fìth* and 'Fìth-fàth' are interchangeable terms and indiscriminately used. They are applied to the occult power which rendered a person invisible to mortal eyes and which transformed one object into another. Men and women were made invisible, or men were transformed into horses, bulls, or stags, while women were transformed into cats, hares, or hinds. These transmutations were sometimes voluntary, sometimes involuntary. The '*fìth-fàth*' was especially serviceable to hunters, warriors, and travellers, rendering them invisible or unrecognisable to enemies and to animals.

*Fath fith Ni mi ort,*
*Le Muire na frithe,*
*Le Bride na brot,*
*Bho chire, bho ruta,*
*Bho mhise, bho bhoc,*
*Bho shionn, 's bho mhac-*
*tire,*
*Bho chrain, 's bho thorc,*
*Bho chu, 's bho chat,*
*Bho mhaghan masaich,*
*Bho chu fasaich,*
*Bho scan foirir,*
*Bho bho, bho mharc,*
*Bho tharbh, bho earc,*
*Bho mhurn, bho mhac,*
*Bho iantaidh an adhar,*
*Bho shnagaidh na talmha,*
*Bho iasgaidh na mara,*
*'S bho shiantaidh na*
*gailbhe.*

*Fath fith* will I make on thee,
By Mary of the augury,
By Bride of the corslet,
From sheep, from ram,
From goat, from buck,
From fox, from wolf,
From sow, from boar,
From dog, from cat,
From hipped-bear,
From wilderness-dog,
From watchful 'scan,'
From cow, from horse,
From bull, from heifer,
From daughter, from son,
From the birds of the air,
From the creeping things of the earth,
From the fishes of the sea,
From the imps of the storm.

Alexander Carmichael. *Carmina Gadelica, Vol I*

# Nightmare Charm or Spell against the *Mara*

Pulling from my head the longest hair it possessed, and then going through the pantomime of binding a refractory- animal, [the nurse] slowly chanted this spell:

*De man o' meicht*
*He rod a' neicht,*
*We nedder swird*
*Nor faerd nor leicht,*
*He socht da mare,*
*He fand da mare,*
*He band da mare*
*Wi' his ain hair,*
*An' made her swear*
*By midder's meicht,*
*Dat sho wad never bide a neicht*
*Whar he had rod, dat man o' meicht."*

**Translation:**

The man of might,

He rode the night,

With shedder sword,

Nor feared or light,

He sought the mare,

He found the mare,

He bound the mare,

With his own hair,

And made her swear.

By midders might,

That she would never bid the night,

Where he has rode, that man of might.

George. F Black. *Orkney and Shetland Islands*

## A Shetland charm against Nightmares

The following charm is given by the charmer Mr. Karl Blind:

> " *Arthur Knight Wi' her ain hair.*
> *He rade a' night, And made da mare*
> *Wi' open swird Ta swear :*
> *An' candle light. 'At she should never*
> *He sought da mare; Bide a' night*
> *He fan' da mare; Whar ever she heard*
> *He bund da mare O' Arthur Knight."*

---

George. F Black. *Orkney and Shetland Islands*

## To rid a house infested with rats or mice

When rats or mice infest a house, a writ of ejectment is stuck upon the wall, which should read thus:

> *Ratton and mouse, Lea the puir woman's house;*
>
> *Gang awa' owre by to the mill, and*
>
> *There ane and a' ye'll get ye fill*

---

Robert Chambers; *Popular Rhymes of Scotland*

# The Consecration of the Cloth

## (*coisrigeadh an aodaich*)

When the women have waulked the cloth, they roll up the web and place it on end in the centre of the frame. They then turn it slowly and deliberately sunwise along the frame, saying with each turn of the web. One can also strike the cloth while chanting or singing:

*Is math a ghabhas mi mo rann,*
*A teurnadh le gleann;*
*Aon rann,*
*Da rann,*
*Tri rann,*
*Ceithir rann,*
*Coig rann,*
*Sia rann,*
*Seachd rann,*
*Seachd gu lath rann*
*Seachd gu lath rann.*

Well can I say my rune,
Descending with the glen;
One rune,
Two runes,
Three runes,
Four runes,
Five runes,
Six runes.
Seven runes,
Seven and a half runes,
Seven and a half runes.

*Nar a gonar fear an eididh,*
*Nar a reubar e gu brath,*
*Cian theid e 'n cath no 'n comhrag,*
*Sgiath chomarach an Domhnach da,*
*Can theid e 'n cath no 'n comhrag,*
*Sgiath chomarach an Domhnach da.*

May the man of this clothing never be wounded,
May torn he never be;
What time he goes into battle or combat,
May the sanctuary shield of the Lord be his.
What time he goes into battle or combat,
May the sanctuary shield of the Lord be his.

*Chan ath-aodach seo, 's chan fhaoigh e,*

This is not second clothing and it is not thigged,
Nor is it the right of sacristan or of

**172**

| | |
|---|---|
| *'S cha chuid cleir no sagairt e.* | priest. |

| | |
|---|---|
| *Biolair uaine ga buain fo* | Cresses green culled beneath a |
| *'S air a toir do mhnai gun* | stone, |
| *fhiosd;* | And given to a woman in secret. |
| *Lurg an fheidh an ceann an* | The shank of the deer in the head of |
| *sgadain,* | the herring, |
| *'S an caol chalp a bhradain* | And in the slender tail of the speckled |
| *bhric.* | salmon. |

Each member of the household for whom the cloth is intended is mentioned by name in the consecration. The cloth is then spat upon, and slowly reversed end by end in the name of Father and of Son and of Spirit till it stands again in the centre of the frame.

---

Alexander Carmichael. *Carmina Gadelica, Vol I*

## A Love Charm

### (*eolas Gradhaich*)

| | |
|---|---|
| *Chan eolas gradhach duit* | It is not love knowledge to thee |
| *Uisge thraghadh tromh shop,* | To draw water through a reed, |
| *Ach gradh an fhir [te] thig* | But the love of him [her] thou choosest, |
| *riut,* | With his warmth to draw to thee. |
| *Le bhlaths a tharsainn ort.* | |

| | |
|---|---|
| | Arise thou early on the day of the |
| *Eirich moth 's an Domhnach,* | Lord, |
| *Gu leac comhnard pleatach* | To the broad flat flag |
| *Beir leat currachd sagart,* | Take with thee the biretta of a |
| *Agus puball beannach.* | priest, [fox-glove (?) |
| | And the pinnacled canopy. [butter-bur |

**173**

*Tog sid air do ghualainn*
*Ann an sluasaid mhaide,*
*Faigh naoi gasa roinnich*
*Air an gearradh le tuaigh,*

*Tri cnamhan seann-duine,*
*Air an tarruinn a uaigh,*
*Loisg iad air teine crionaich,*
*Is dean gu leir 'n an luath.*

*Crath an dearbh*
*bhrollach do leannain,*
*An aghaidh gath gaoth tuath,*
*'S theid mis an rath, 's am*
*baran duit,*
*Nach falbh am fear [bean] sin*
*uat.*

(?)

Lift them on thy shoulder
In a wooden shovel,
Get thee nine stems of ferns
Cut with an axe,

The three bones of an old man,
That have been drawn from the grave,
Burn them on a fire of faggots,
And make them all into ashes.

Shake it in the very breast of thy
lover,
Against the sting of the north wind,
And I will pledge, and warrant thee,
That man [woman] will never leave thee.

---

Alexander Carmichael. *Carmina Gadelica, Vol II*

## To settle the winds at sea

In Orkney, when a boat was leaving port and the wind ahead, the wife turned her petticoats [inside-out] to turn the wind round. The same rite was observed if the boats were expected home from whale fishing or from a foreign voyage, and the wind was against them. Sweethearts used to turn their petticoats and go down to the sea and sing: -

*O blaw, ye winds, sae fair and Free*
*Back, back my ain dear lad to me:*
*It's—fir his name I daurna tell—*
*But bring him back I lo'e so well.*

---

J. M. McPherson. *Primitive Beliefs in the North-East of Scotland*

174

# To secure a good harvest

The wise woman and farmers wife, Jonet Wishart combined the ritual of throwing stones with partial nudity, to secure a good harvest. She was charged with having, in harvest, gone to her own Gudeman's croft, called Round About, and there taken all her clothes about her head, being naked from waist down. She then took a great number of stones and going backwards cast one part behind her over her head, and the other part forward. It was a rite no doubt intended to avert barrenness and secure prosperity for her land.

J. M. McPherson; *'Primitive Beliefs in the North-East of Scotland'*.

# The New Moon

## *(A' Ghealach Ur)*

To sea-faring people like those of the Western Isles the light and guidance of the moon is a matter of much interest and importance, often indeed a matter of life or death. Sun, moon and stars are all addressed for practical purposes. The moon was of more concern than the sun, for by day, whether the sun was visible or not, the people could thread their way
through their intricate tortuous reefs and rocks, fords and channels. But they could not do this on a moonless night except at the peril of their lives.
This is one reason for the many odes and hymns addressed to the gracious luminary of the night.

*Fàilte dhut, a ghealach ùr,*
*Àilleagan iùil na bàidh !*
*Ta mi lùbadh dhut mo ghlùn,*
*Ta mi curnadh dhut mo ghràidh.*
*Ta mi lùbadh dhut mo ghlùn,*
*Ta mi tiubhradh dhut mo làmh,*

*Ta mi togail dhut mo shùil,*
*A ghealach ùr nan tràth.*
*Fàilte dhut, a ghealach ùr,*
*A mhuirneag mo ghràidh !*
*Fàilte dhut, a ghealach ùr,*
*A mhuirneag nan gràs !*

*Tha thu siubhal 'na do chùrs,*
*Tha thu stiùradh nan Ian ;*
*Tha thu soillseadh dhuinn do ghnùis,*
*A ghealach ùr nan tràth.*
*A rioghainn an iùil,*
*A rioghainn an àigh,*
*A rioghainn mo ruin,*
*A ghealach ùr nan tràth !*

**Translates:**

Hail to thee, thou new moon,
Guiding jewel of gentleness !
I am bending to thee my knee,
I am offering thee my love.
I am bending to thee my knee,
I am giving thee my hand,
I am lifting to thee mine eye,
O new moon of the seasons.
Hail to thee, thou new moon,
Joyful maiden of my love !
Hail to thee, thou new moon.
Joyful maiden of the graces !
Thou art travelling in thy course.
Thou art steering the full tides ;
Thou art illuming to us thy face,
O new moon of the seasons.

**176**

Thou queen-maiden of guidance.
Thou queen-maiden of good fortune,
Thou queen-maiden my beloved,
Thou new moon of the seasons!

---

Alexander Carmichael. *Carmina Gadelica Vols III*

## The Sun Prayer

### (*An Urnaigh Ghrèine*)

When the sun would rise on the tops of the peaks, he would put off his head-covering and he would bow down his head, giving glory to the great God of life for the glory of the sun and for the goodness of its light to the children of men and to the animals of the world. When the sunset in the western ocean the old man would again take off his head-covering, and he would bow his head to the ground

This incantation was recited by John MacNeill, cottar, Buaile nam Bodach (The old man of Barra):

> *Fàilte ort fein, a ghrian nan tràth,*
> *'S tu siubhal ard nan speur ;*
> *Do cheumaibh treun air sgeith nan ard,*
> *'S tu màthair àigh nan reul.*
> *Thu laighe sios an cuan na dìth*
> *Gun diobhail is gun sgàth ;*
> *Thu 'g eirigh suas air stuagh na sith,*
> *Mar rioghainn òg fo bhlàth.*

**Translates:**

> Hail to thee, thou sun of the seasons,
> As thou traversest the skies aloft ;

**177**

Thy steps are strong on the wing of the heavens,
Thou art the glorious mother of the stars.
Thou liest down in the destructive ocean
Without impairment and without fear ;
Thou risest up on the peaceful wave-crest
Like a queenly maiden in bloom.

---

Alexander Carmichael. *Carmina Gadelica Vol. III*

## MacPherson's spells for summoning winds

Macpherson of power' (Mac-Mhuirich nam buadh), a noted wizard in South Uist, was on a passage by sea on a calm day. The skipper said to him, "Ask for a wind, Mac-Vuirich." He did so, saying:

> *"An east wind from the calm aether,*
> *As the Lord of the elements has ordained,*
> *A wind that needs not rowing nor reefing,*
> *That will do nought deceitful to us."*

"Weak and trifling you have asked it," said the skipper, "when I am at the helm." Mac-Vuirich answered:

> *"A north wind hard as a rod,*
> *Struggling above our gunwale,*
> *Like a red roe sore pressed,*
> *Descending a hillock's narrow hard head."*

"It does not attain to praise yet," said the skipper, and Mac-Vuirich went on:

> *'If there be a wind in cold hell,*
> *Devil; send it after us,*
> *In waves and surges;*
> *And if one go ashore, let it be I,*

*And if two, I and my dog."*

A sea came, that rolled the boat's stern over her bows, and all were drowned but Mac-Vuirich and his dog.

**Another:**

The power of this wizard over the elements was also shown on another occasion. The MacRanalds were coming to attack the MacNeills of Barra, to whom Mac-Vuirich was favourable. Their boat was seen coming along the wild and rocky coast on the west of Skye, and was sunk by the mighty wizard uttering the following words:

> *A south-west wind toward Eiste point,*
> *Mist and rain,*
> *Clan Ranald on a breaking board,*
> *I reck it not;*
> *A narrow unsteady vessel,*
> *A lofty pointed sail,*
> *A lading of empty barrels,*
> *And bilge-water to the thwarts,*
> *A weak irascible crew*
> *Having no respect one for another.*

As might be expected, such a boat did not go far before sinking.

---

John Gregorson Campbell. *Witchcraft & second sight in the Highlands & Islands*

# A charm to win in court.

The litigant went at morning dawn to a place where three streams met. And as the rising sun gilded the mountain crests, the man placed his two palms edgeways together and filled them with water from the junction of the streams. Dipping his face into this improvised basin, he fervently repeated the prayer, after which he made his way to the court, feeling strong in the justice of his cause. On entering the court and on looking round the room, the applicant for justice mentally, sometimes in an undertone, said

| | |
|---|---|
| *Dhe, seun an teach* | God sain the house |
| *Bho steidh gu fraigh;* | From site to summit; |
| *M' fheart os cinn gach neach,* | My word above every person, |
| *Feart gach neach fo m'* | The word of every person below my |
| *thraigh.'* | foot. |

The ceremonies observed in saying these prayers for justice, like those observed on many similar occasions, are symbolic. The bathing represents purification; the junction of three streams, the union of the Three Persons of the Godhead; and the spreading rays of the morning sun, divine grace. The deer is symbolic of wariness, the horse of strength, the serpent of wisdom, and the king of dignity.

---

Mackenzie, William. *Gaelic Incantations, Charms and Blessing of the Hebrides*

# Invocation for Justice

## (*ora ceartais*)

*Ionnlaidh mise m' aodann*
*'S na naodh gatha greine,*
*Mar a dh' ionnlaid Moire a Mac*
*Am bainne brat na breine.*

*Gaol a bhi 'na m' aodann,*
*Caomh a bhi 'na m' ghnuis,*
*Caora meala 'na mo theanga,*
*M' anail mar an tuis.*

**180**

*Is dubh am bail ud thall,*
*Is dubh daoine th' ann;*
*Is mis an eala bhan,*
*Banruinn os an ceann.*

*Falbhaidh mi an ainme Dhe,*
*An riochd feidh, an riochd each,*
*An riochd nathrach, an riochd righ:*
*Is treasa liom fin na le gachneach.*

**Translates:**

I Will wash my face
In the nine rays of the sun,
As Mary washed her Son
In the rich fermented milk.
Love be in my countenance,
Benevolence in my mind,
Dew of honey in my tongue,
My breath as the incense.
Black is yonder town,
Black are those therein,
I am the white swan,
Queen above them.
I will travel in the name of God,
In likeness of deer, in likeness of horse,
In likeness of serpent, in likeness of king:
Stronger will it be with me than with all persons.

Like the *fith-fath* charm, animals are employed in this charm to magically obtain the powerful attributes of these animals upon you. Attaining a successful end-iron, symbolic of hardiness and endurance; a horse, of strength; the serpent, of cunning; and the deer, swiftness; the king, of dignity. Ending with "*Stronger will it be with me than with all persons*" as to mean the strength of those mentioned in this charm will

**181**

be stronger within you than anyone else in this case the members of the courthouse and jury.

---

Alexander Carmichael. *Carmina Gadelica Vols I*

## A spell for the Faces of Young Women

> *Bounty is in thy countenance,*
> *The Son of God succour thee*
> *From the evil men of the world,*
> *The vigil of loving St. Mary keep thee,*
> *A smooth modest tongue be in thy head,*
> *Fair hair in thy two eyebrows,*
> *Fin, the son of Cuäl, between these;*
> *Since it be Mary and her Son*
> *That gave them that charm,*
> *May the taste of honey be*
> *On every word you say,*
> *To commons and to nobles,*
> *Upon this and each day*
> *To the end of the year.*

---

John Gregorson Campbell. *Witchcraft & second sight in the Highlands & Islands*

## Against Drowning and in War.

A native of the Island of Coll, who served in the British army from the taking of Copenhagen, throughout the Peninsular and continental wars, and only died this year (1874), a most kind-hearted and powerfully built man, attributed his safe return from the wars in some measure to having learned this charm in his youth:

> *The charm Mary put round her Son,*

*And Bridget put in her banners,*

*And Michael put in his shield,*

*And the Son of God before His throne of clouds;*

*A charm art thou against arrow,*

*A charm art thou against sword,*

*A charm against the red-tracked bullet;*

*An island art thou in the sea,*

*A rock art thou on land;*

*And greater be the fear these have*

*Of the body, round which the charm goes,*

*In presence of Colum-Kil*

*With his mantle round thee.*

---

John Gregorson Campbell. *Witchcraft & second sight in the Highlands & Islands*

# SCOTTISH DIVINATION AND FORTUNE-TELLING

## Gaelic rhyme of evil omens

*'Chunnaic mi selicheag air lar lom;*
*Chunnaic mi searrach is earball rium;*
*Chac a chubhac air mo cheann;*
*Is dh' aithnich mi rachadh a bhlian' ad lium.'*

**Translates:**

'I saw a snail on bare ground;
I saw a foal with his tail towards me;
I heard the cuckoo before breaking fast;
And I knew that that year would not go with me.'

---

Donald Masson. *Notes from the North highlands*

## The *Frith*

The '*frith*' (augury), was a species of divination enabling the '*frithir*,' augurer, to see into the unseen. This divination was made to ascertain the position and condition of the absent and the lost and was applied to man and beast. The augury was made on the first Monday of the quarter and immediately before sunrise. The Augurer, fasting, and with bare feet, bare head, and closed eyes, went to the doorstep and placed a hand on each jamb. Mentally beseeching the God of the unseen to show him his quest and to grant him his augury, the Augurer opened his eyes and looked steadfastly straight in front of him. From the nature and position of the objects within his sight, he drew his conclusions.

Many men in the Highlands and Islands were famed augurers, and many stories, realistic, romantic, and extremely curious, are still told of their divinations. As already mentioned, the Gaelic term for a female seer or fortune-seer is *cailleach nam frìth* which roughly translates as the "old woman who can perform augury" or even the *Frith* rite.

The people say that the Virgin made an augury when Christ was missing, and that it was by means of this augury that Mary and Joseph ascertained that Christ was in the Temple disputing with the doctors. Hence this divination is called *frith Mhoire*, the augury of Mary; and *frithireachd Mhoire*, the auguration of Mary.

The 'frith' of the Celt is akin to the '*frett*' of the Norseman. Probably the surnames Freer, Frere, are modifications of '*frithir*,' augurer. Persons bearing this name claim that their progenitors were astrologers to the kings of Scotland.

*Dia faram, Dia fodham,*
*Dia romham, Dia am*
*dheoghainn,*
*Mis air do shlighe Dhia,*
*Thus, a Dhia, air mo luirg.*

God over me, God under me,
God before me, God behind me,
I on Thy path, O God,
Thou, O God, in my steps.

*Frith rinn Muire d'a Mac,*
*Iobair Bride ri a glac,*
*Am fac thu i, a Righ nan dul?--*
*Ursa Righ nan dul gum fac.*

The augury made of Mary to her Son,
The offering made of Bride through her palm,
Sawest Thou it, King of life? --
Said the King of life that He saw.

*Frith Muire da muirichinn fein,*
*Trath dha bhi re ri cuairt,*
*Fios firinn gun fios breuige,*
*Gum faic mi fein na bheil uam.*

The augury made by Mary for her own offspring,
When He was for a space a missing,
Knowledge of truth, not knowledge of falsehood,
That I shall truly see all my quest.

*Mac Muire min-ghil, Righ nan*
*dul,*

| | |
|---|---|
| *A shulachadh domh-s' na bheil uam,* | Son of beauteous Mary, King of life, |
| *Le gras nach falnaich, mu m' choinneamh,* | Give Thou me eyes to see all my quest, With grace that shall never fail, before me, |
| *Gu brath nach smalaich 's nach doillich.* | That shall never quench nor dim. |

## Making the *Frith*

A Frith may be made at any time; but the first Monday of the quarter, *a' chiad Di-luain de'n Raith* is considered the most auspicious. The mode of making the Frith is as follows:

In the morning the Ave Maria, or Beannachadh Moire, is said thus—

> *Beannaichear dhut, a Mhoire,*
> *Tha thu lan dhe na grasan;*
> *Tha 'n Tighearna maille riut;*
> *'S beannuichte thu measg nam ban;*
> *'S beannaichte toradh do bhronn Iosa.*
> *A Naomh Mhoire, 'Mhathair Dhe*
> *Guidh air ar son-ne, na peacaich,*
> *A nis agus aig uair ar bais-Amen.*

**Translated:**

> Blessed are you, Mary,
> You are full of Grace;
> The Lord is with you;
> Blessed art thou among women;
> Blessed is the fruit of your womb- Jesus
> Holy Mary, Mother of God
> Pray for us, sinners,
> Now and at the hour of our death—Amen.

**187**

After repeating the Ave, the person proceeds with closed eyes to the door. On reaching the *maide-buinn*, or doorstep, he opens his eyes, and if he sees the Cross (*Crois Chriosda*), although it was only made with two straws' lying across each other, it is a sign that all will be well. On getting outside, he proceeds round the house sunwise (deiseal), repeating the following Incantation:

*Dia romham ;*
*Moire am dheaghaidh*
*'S am Mac a thug Righ nan Dul*
*'S a chairich Brighde na glaic.*
*Mis' air do shlios, a Dhia,*
*Is Dia na'm luirg.*
*Mac Moire, a's Righ nan Dul,*
*A shoillseachadh gach ni dheth so,*
*Le a ghras, mu'm choinneamh.*

**Translates:**

God before me;
The Virgin Mary after me;
And the Son sent by the King of the Elements;
And whom St Bridget took in her arms.
I am on thy land, 0 God!
And God on my footsteps;
May the Son of Mary, King of the Elements,
Reveal the meaning of each of these things
Before me, through His grace.

Another version of the Incantation is as follows:

*Tha mise falbh air srath Chriosd :*
*Dia romham, Dia am dheighidh,*

*A's Dia a m' luirg.1*
*A Fhrith a rinn Moire dha 'Mac,*
*A sheid Brighde troimh a glaic,*
*Mar a fhuair ise fios firinneach,*
*Gun fhios breige,*
*Mise dh' fhaicinn samhla's coltas*

**Translates:**

I go forth on the track of Chris
God before me, God behind me,
And God on my footsteps.
The Frith that Mary made for her Son,
Which Bridget blew through her palm;
And as she got a true response,
Without a false one,
May I behold the likeness and similitude of
[name]

The Incantation finished, the person looks forth over the country, and by the auguries or omens which meet the eye he divines what will be the fate of the man or animal for whom the *Frith* is being made— whether the absent one, about whom nothing is known, is in life, and well; or whether the sick man or beast at home will recover from his ailment. Subjoined is a list of objects, with their significance.

## The Omen-reading of the *Frith*

Here is a list of omen reading of the *Frith* complied by William Mackenzie with the help of a gentleman named Allan Macdonald (Dalibrog, South Uist):

## lucky (*Rathadach*)

- A man, especially with brown hair, is considered to be a good sign.
- A man coming towards or looking in the direction of the seer is considered to be an excellent sign.
- A man standing, or an animal rising, indicates that the person the frìth is being performed for will soon recover from the sickness they have been suffering from
- A woman with brown or dark hair is a good sign (brown is considered to be the best)
- A woman standing is an excellent sign.
- A woman passing by or coming towards the seer is a neutral sign.
- A cock coming towards or looking in the direction of the seer is an excellent sign.
- A bird coming towards the seer indicates news – especially a letter on its way.
- A bird, including one mid-flight, is generally a good sign (with some exceptions), but especially the dove or pigeon (McNeill notes only the dove and lark)[23]
- A duck is an especially good sign for sailors, signifying they will be kept safe from drowning.
- A dog, horse (with the exception of a chestnut or red horse),[24] foal, calf, lamb are all good signs if they are facing towards the seer
- A sheep, lamb or calf is especially good if the person enquiring is about to go on a journey, so long as they are facing you.

## Unlucky (*Rosadach*)

- *A man* going away is an unlucky sign
- A man lying down indicates illness, or the continued suffering from an illness
- A man digging over the earth signifies death[25]
- An animal lying down indicates death

- A woman standing is unlucky – death or an untoward event
- A woman passing is not so bad[26]
- A woman with light-red or fair hair is unlucky
- A woman with deep-red hair is a very unlucky sign
- A sparrow indicates the death of a child ("Three or four of these always come before the death of a child, and return each day until the death, not reappearing after it.")
- Chickens without a cockrel, crows and rooks are all unlucky signs, especially if they are approaching the seer
- A crow or raven signifies a death
- Ducks or hens with their heads held low signifies death, and the more that can be seen holding themselves in such a manner, the speedier and more certain the death is[27]
- A pig with its back to the seer is an unlucky sign, for everyone but Campbells, but if the pig is facing the seer it is neutral[28]
- The cat is an unlucky sign, suggesting witchcraft, for all but those of the Clann Chatain (which includes Mackintoshes and Macphersons)
- A chestnut or red horse signifies death.
- A goat is a bad sign, especially if the enquirer is about to go on a journey – the journey should be postponed.

---

Alexander Carmichael. *Carmina Gadelica, Vol II*
William Mackenzie. *Gaelic Incantations, Charms and Blessing of the Hebrides*

## Shoulder-blade of Sheep.
### *(Slinneanachd)*

The shoulder-blades of sheep are used in the Highlands for predicting of marriages, births, deaths, and funerals. To be effective the flesh must be removed without the use of any iron, consequently no knife or fork must touch it. When cleaned properly, one person held it over his left shoulder, and another looked through the thin part of the broad end of the bone, below the ridge.

In Lewis divination by means of the blade-bone of a sheep was practised in the following manner. The shoulder-blade of a black sheep was procured by the inquirer into future events, and with this he went to see some reputed seer, who held the bone lengthwise before him and in the direction of the greatest length of the island. In this position the seer began to read the bone from some marks that he saw in it, and then oracularly declared what events to individuals or families were to happen. It is not very far distant that there were a host of believers in this method of prophecy.

R. C. Maclagan. *Notes on Folklore Objects Collected in Argyleshire*
John Abercromby. *Traditions, Customs and Superstitions of the Lewis*

## Brunt Stanes

A curious divination rite performed by certain Scottish cunning folk was the use of three stones to determine whether a kirk-spirit, hill-spirit or a water-spirit had caused a patient harm. The rite was not only divinatory but also curative in nature. Such stones were sometimes referred to as 'Brunt' stones. Brunt being Scots for "Burnt" which according to as J.M. McPherson:

> "brunt" stones, frequently immersed in water. To burned stones were ascribed many of the virtues attributed to iron. Like iron, they impregnated the water and imparted to it magical powers.

A wise woman of Elgin Janet Hossack (1650) would cure a child by taking stones from a stream where the quick (living) and dead passed over, she burnt the stones on a fire and put them in water wherewith she washed the child. She casted the stones back into the stream and the child recovered.

The use of Brunt stones was mentioned in the witch trials of Catherine Caray (3rd July 1616) and Katherine Craigie (1643) which by their accounts seemed to be used to divine what spirits had caused the illness and cure it them at the same time. Catherine Caray (1616) description in her confessions of three stones that she used to determine whether an illness came from *"ane of the spirit of the hill, ane for the kirk-yeard and ane for the sey"* which she concluded it was a *sey* (sea) spirit that was the cause. A similar was used by Katherine Craigie (1643), the wise woman of Rousay (Orkeny) who described the 'Brunt stane' rite in most detail:

Katherine Graige went to Janet's house before the day (sunrise) and brought with her three stones which she put the [hearth] fire and left them there all day until sunset, and then took them out of the fire and put them under the threshold all night until the next sunrise. Then with a vessel of water she put the stones in one after another which Janet heard them *cherme and churle* in the water, which Katherine concluded it was a kirk-spirit which troubled her husband Robbie (Robert). She then directed Janet to wash her husband with the water the three stones had been in, and to repeat the rite Katherine had performed a further two more times, washing her husband with the water. By the third night her husband was cured.

Katherine could tell which spirit had troubled her sisters' husband by the way which the stone *cherme and churle*—moved and make a noise. When I have performed this kind of divination by Brunt stones, I was able to determine what spirit that was responsible by other observations such as bubbles came from the stone or if it simply acted weirdly to the others. To distinguish from which stone is which, you can mark them with signs or symbols representing each of the three spirits. The ones that I use have been taken from their locations; one from a graveyard to represent the Kirk-spirit, from a hilltop-*Hill-spirit*, and a from a loch-*water-spirit*. I have known some Scottish practitioners to use stones found of different coloured stones, but it is completely your choice what and how you decide to use them.

Also, I may add that in Katherine's confession she said she used this rite on another occasion to heal her other sister's husband Thomas of sickness which this time was a water-spirit which troubled him. This time, by the third application she washed her husband beside a loch, all the while traveling to and performing the rite by the loch in silence. This could indicate that whatever spirit that troubled the person, the spirit's power over the person must returned to its domain place by washing or pouring the water over the person head on a hill, graveyard or beside a body of water. Often in folk magic when you do this kind of work the patient and practitioner is instructed is to walk onwards and do not look back.

McPherson provides an explanation on how Brunt stones were also used in divining what part of the body where a disease laid:

> Three stones were taken, sometimes from a ford or bridge over which the living and the dead passed. Sometimes they were stones in the possession of a charmer. These stones represent the head, the heart, and the body, and were so named. Placed overnight amongst the hot ashes on the hearth, they were taken up in the morning and dropped one by one into a basin of water. The stone which gave out the loudest sound as it came in contact with the water, showed the part of the body where the disease lay.

The spirits themselves could also represent more deeper meanings; a kirk-spirit, the spirits of the dead/ancestors at the middle worlds, Hill-spirit; the spirits above and the Water-spirit; the spirits below. I have seen the three stones being represented by the Celtic reconstructionist theology of land, sea, and Sky.

---

J. M. McPherson. *Primitive Beliefs in the North-East of Scotland*

*Miscellany of the Abbotsford Club Vol.I.* Edinburgh Printing Company (1837)

# Divining Staves

There is a Gaelic method of 'casting the lots' I came up with based on Irish myth of Dalan and Eochaiod Airem, where Dalan, the druid of Eochaiod Airem, who took four rods of yew and wrote Oghams on them, and by the means in which he threw them down, was the keys of his seership had discovered that Eochaiod's Queen whereabouts was in Fairyland.

Now, a pre-created set isn't necessary for this divining method, but you can make yourself a set if you wish. Go to a yew tree nearest to you, go on bent knee and pray to the Yew tree to bestow upon you, through its wisdom to aid you in your quest of divining your question at mind. Then from its bough, cut a long thin branch with your pocketknife, divide it in four and shave the bark off at one side of each stave. With your knife or a pen, scribe onto each yew stave the ogham; Iodhadh (Yew), *Eadhadh* (Test-tree), *Úr* (Earth/soil), and *Ruis* (red, redness).

I use this ogham in praise of the yew tree that bore the staves, the test-tree or divining tree for divination, the Earth for its aid, and red, the colour presenting life-force and power. Once prepared, I ask my question and throw them down. You can ask the Irish deity Ogma for his aid in this if you wish. The genuine rule of thumb as a simple interpretation of the oracle is; a $X$ is a negative answer, + a positive, and staves largely spaced apart from each other is a 'Maybe' or uncertain answer. Other methods of personal divinatory interpretation can of course be applied to this way of throwing down the stave.

You may notice, if you are familiar to the Ogham divination practice that some of the ogham do not correspond to trees as usually seen today. This is because the Irish Gaelic words do not translate as they are portrayed by the modern Ogham divination.

The modern New Age and Neopagan approaches to ogham largely derive from the now-discredited theories of Robert Graves in his book; *The White Goddess* and who had appropriated the names of Ogham to suit his system of the Celtic "Tree Alphabet".

## Swimming of Names

The 'Swimming of names or *Hydromancy*, was a divination method to find out who had bewitched you or in some case, the recovery of lost money. Names of the suspected would be written on separate pieces of name and placed into a basin of water, and the first to sink was the suspected curser or witch. McPherson explains a case of the rite being performed in Fraserburgh:

> Alexander Fraser in the township of Kinbog confessed that, at the desire of John Philip, "who wanted ane serk," he had written the names of all the people of Kinbog on piece of water and therefore cast the papers into water "to try the thift supposing that be guilty peresone whose name did sink."

The rite seemed to resemble the horrific witch test known as swimming the witch, coming from the folk belief that water rejects the guilty, or in this case, the "sacred water rejects the innocent". It is uncertain how the rite was used to recover lost money, but my profession guess would be writing the names of places or areas where the person might have lost the money.

---

J. M. McPherson. *Primitive Beliefs in the North-East of Scotland*

## The Ordeal of the Grave

The Ordeal of the Grave was a rite to find out if a sickly infant would live or die, it was presented to the grave. The charmer or Wise Man/Woman would dig two small shallow graves, the one named the living grave and the other the dead. The suffer was laid between the two graves, whilst saying "Gog send it health or Heaven" and if the infant turned towards the Living Grave it would recover but if the Dead Grave the bairn would die. If the infant was too ill to move, the graves would be named as before and the parent asked to place the bairn into the grave of her choosing, and the one that the father or mother placed the bairn in would be the result of if the bairn would live or die.

The rite a similar rite was used in Shetland in the belief that the ailing child was a Changeling, and a consequent effort was made to get back the true child. The dwining Changeling was left in the one grave and the other grave was awaiting the parents' own progeny.

---

J. M. McPherson. *Primitive Beliefs in the North-East of Scotland*

# Divination for lovers

In twenty-eight rhymed stanzas (*Halloween*, 1786) Rober Burns describes how "some merry, friendly, country folks" convened on Halloween to perform various traditional rituals, with the hope of thus conjuring up images of their future marriage partners. Each ritual, described in Scottish dialect, is elucidated with an explanatory footnote.

*Note to Stanza 4:*

The first ceremony of Halloween, is, pulling each a Stock or plant of kail. They must go out, hand in hand, with eyes shut, and pull the first they meet with: its being big or little, straight, or crooked, is prophetic of the size and shape of the grand object of all their Spells - - the husband or wife. If any yird, or earth, stick to the root, that is tocher, or fortune; and the taste of the cufloc, that is, the heart of the stem, is indicative of the natural temper and disposition. Lastly, the stems, or to give them their ordinary appellation, the runts, are placed somewhere above the head of the door; and the Christian names of the people whom chance brings into the house, are, according to the priority of placing the runts, the names in question.

*Note to Stanza 6:*

They go to the barn-yard, and pull each, at three several times, a stalk of Oats. If the third stalk wants the top-pickle, that is, the grain at the top of the stalk, the party in question will want the Maidenhead.

*Note to Stanza 7:*

Burning the nuts is a favourite charm. They name the lad and lass to each particular nut, as they lay them in the fire; and according as they burn quietly together, or start from beside one another, the course and issue of the Courtship will be.

*Note to Stanza 11:*

Whoever would, with success, try this spell (*Winning o' the blue clew*), must strictly observe these directions. Steal out, all alone, to the kiln, and, darkling, throw into the pot, a clew (thread) of blue yarn; wind it in a new clew off the old one; and towards the latter end, something will hold the thread: demand, "wha hands?" i. e. who holds? and answer will be returned from the kiln pot, by naming the Christian and surname of your future Spouse.

*Note to Stanza 13:*

Take a candle, and go, alone, to a looking glass: eat an apple before it, and some traditions say you should comb your hair all the time: the face of your conjugal companion, to be, will be seen in the glass, as if peeping over your shoulder.

*Note to Stanza 16:*

Steal out, unperceived, and sow a handful of hemp seed; harrowing it with anything you can conveniently draw after you. Repeat, now and then, "Hemp seed I saw thee, Hemp seed I saw thee; and him (or her) that is to be my true love, I come after me and pou thee." Look over your left shoulder, and you will see the appearance of the person invoked, in the attitude of pulling hemp. Some traditions say, "come after me and shaw thee," that is, show thyself; in which case it simply appears. Others omit the harrowing, and say, "come after me and harrow thee."

*Note to Stanza 21:*

This charm must likewise be performed, unperceived and alone. You go to the barn, and open both doors; taking them off the hinges, if possible; for there is danger, that the Being, about to appear, may shut the doors, and do you some mischief. Then take that instrument used in winnowing the corn, which, in our country dialect, we call a wecht; and go through all the attitudes of letting down corn against the wind. Repeat it three times; and the third time, an apparition will pass through the barn, in at the windy door, and out at the other, having both the figure in question and the appearance or retinue, marking the employment or station in life.

*Note to Stanza 23:*

Take an opportunity of going, unnoticed, to a Bear-stack, and fathom it three times round. The last fathom of the last time, you will catch in your arms, the appearance of your future conjugal yoke-fellow.

*Note to Stanza 24:*

You go out, one or more, for this is a social spell, to a south-running spring or rivulet, where "three Lairds' lands meet," and dip your left shirt-sleeve. Go to bed in sight of a fire and hang your wet sleeve before it to dry. Ly awake; and sometime near midnight, an apparition, having the exact figure of the grand object in question, will come and turn the sleeve, as if to dry the other side of it.

*Note to Stanza 27:*

Take three dishes; put clean water in one, foul water in another, and leave the third empty: blindfold a person, and lead him to the hearth where the dishes are ranged; he (or she) dips the left hand: if by chance in the clean water, the future husband or wife will come to the bar of Matrimony, a Maid; if in the foul, a widow; if in the empty dish, it foretells, with equal certainty, no marriage at all. It is repeated three times; and every time the arrangement of the dishes is altered.

Edited and commented by Ash William Mills; Robert Burns. *Poems, Chiefly in the Scottish Dialect*

# THE
# Spaewife;
### OR, UNIVERSAL
# FORTUNE-TELLER.

##### WHEREIN YOUR

## FUTURE WELFARE MAY BE KNOWN,

###### BY

## *Physiognomy—Cards—Palmistry— and Coffee Grounds.*

###### ALSO,

## A DISTINCT TREATISE ON MOLES.

---

## *BY AN ASTROLOGER.*

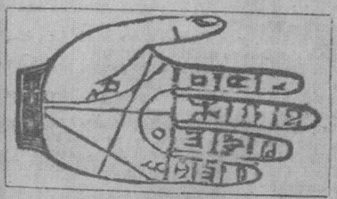

## KILMARNOCK:
*Printed by H. Crawford, Bookseller.*
### 1827.

The following chapbook on fortune-telling was so popular during 19<sup>th</sup> century Scotland that were was several published editions. Firstly, in Kilmarnock, then later in Edinburgh, Glasgow, Falkirk, and Aberdeen.

The material supplied is of public domain and a Digital transcript can view online by:

The National Library of Scotland, Edinburgh https://digital.nls.uk/

Digital transcript; Edited by Ash William Mills (2021)

Link: https://digital.nls.uk/108602623

Shelfmark: L.C.2855(14)

The

# Spaewife;

OR, Universal

## FORTUNE-TELLER:

wherein your

FUTURE WELFARE MAY BE KNOWN,

By

*Physiognomy—Cards—Palmistry—
and Coffee Grounds.*

Also,

A DISTINCT TREATISE ON MOLES.

———

*BY AN ASTROLOGER.*

———

KILMARNOCK:

*Printed by H. Crawford, Bookseller,*

1827.

# THE
# FORTUNE-TELLER.

_____

## SECRET INDICATIONS.

*Judgments to be drawn from the Hairt (Heart) according to the substance and colour.*

The hair is one of the most beautiful natural ornaments that adorn the head of man or woman.

The Apostle Paul permits women to wear long hair as an advancement to their beauty and to be pleasing in the eyes of their husbands.

1. Hair that is soft and thick denotes a man of much mildness. #

2. When the hair hangs down and is soft, rt denotes the body to decline to dryness.

3. Much hair denotes a hot person, and that he is soon angry.

4. Abundance of hair in young children shews that they increase in melancholy.

5. Cut led hair and black, denotes heat; the people of the South have it most part alike.

6. Hair standing up an end, like the prickles of a hedge-hog, signifies a fearful person, and of ill courage.

## Colour of the Hair.

1, White hair signifies great frigidity or cold, as may be seen in old men: but many people after much sickness, or trouble of mind, will on a sudden find their hair turn grey or white, as also after a fright or disappointment. A French Officer, aged 23, on a sudden received sentence of death; the news had such an effect on him, that before morning his hair was changed to milk white.

2. Black hair shews a person very amorous, but cruel and ungenerous.

3. Hair the colour of gold, shews a treacherous person, arbitrary and proud.

4. Dark red hair has the same signification. The perspiration of a red haired person is disagreeable.

5. Chestnut-coloured hair, or dark brown, denotes a fair, just, free, and liberal person.

## The Beard.

1 • A thin, soft beard shews a person lustful, effeminate, of a trader body, fearful and inconstant.

2. A red beard denotes the person courteous and friendly, a great flatterer, and very soon angry.

3. A dark beard is good, yet it denotes a person maybe cordial, sincere, thoughtful, and bold.

4. He that hath a decent beard, handsome, and thick of hair, is good natured and reasonable.


### The Chin.


1. A long chin, denotes the person angry, and importunate in the use of words.

2. A little chin shews inveteracy and malice.
3. A round and thin chin is not manly, but womanish, and signifies boldness and much pride.

4. A square chin is manly, and denotes much courage and strength of body; and such persons are commonly given to words.

5. A round chin Anci 'dimpled shews good nature, but much addicted to pleasure.

6. A lean wrinkled chin represents a cold, impotent, and malicious person.

### The Eye-brows and Eye-lids.

1. A person a having much, and long hair on the eye-brows, and both join across the nose, is a very simple person, but conceited in his own opinion colour.

2. When the eye-brows are short and narrow, denote the man good-natured and reasonable.

3. The eye-lids short and small, are thought wise and secret, yet covetous of great matters.

4. When the eye-lids are long, and long hair or the eye-lashes, they signify a person of low capacity, and false in his dealings.

### The Neck

1. He or she that hath a long neck, is of a simple nature, not secret, fearfully unlearned, a glutton, and great drinker in general.

2. He that hath a neck short and small, is wise, but deceitful, secret, constant, discreet, yet passionate and ingenious.

3. He that hath the neck fat and fleshy, is proud, wherefore he is compared to a bull, who is always ready to be angry.

4. A small neck denotes a weak understanding; if a female, she will be much inclined to sickness, and gnawing of the stomach.

5. A neck inclined to the right side, denotes prudence, generosity, and curious in studies; but inclined to the left side, declares vice and impudicity.

### The Eyes.

1. Great eyes denote a slothful, bold, and lying person, of a rustic and course mind.

2. Eyes deep in the head, denote a great mind, yet full of doubts, but generous and friendly

3- Little eyes, like those of a mole or pig, denote a weak understanding, and easily imposed.

4. Beware of squint eyes, for out of one hundred you will not find two faithfuls. It is very ill luck to meet a squinting person.

5 Eyes that move slowly, or look sleepy, denote an unfaithful and slothful person.

6. The worst of all the eyes are the yellowish or citron—-beware of them, for the possessor is a dangerous person, if yon jure in his power.

7. Beware also of them, who, when they speak, twinkle their eyes, for they are double-minded. If are a woman that doth so with her left eye, trust or not as to the faithfulness of her love but you will seldom find deceit where the eye looks with a modest confidence, not staring you out of Countenance, nor averting as if detected of a crime—but when in business, love, or friendship, mere appears a tender firmness.

### The Nose

1. A long nose denotes a vain mind, unruly disposition, much given to wrangling, and not to be depended on.

2. A high nose denotes a violent person, a vain liar, and extremely lascivious, easily believing another and very inconstant.

3. He that hath a big nose every way, long and hanging down, is covetous in everything.

4-. When the nose is crooked, signifies a proud man, and him or her is never good, but justice overtakes them.

5. He that hath the nose hairy at or above the point, is a person altogether simple-hearted.

6. A Roman or aquiline nose denotes a haughty, arbitrary, and wranglesome (argumentative) person.

7. A nose that is round and long, of a pleasant feature, besides being one of the perfections of beauty, denotes the woman or maid, wise, prudent, and chaste-; particularly if she has blue eyes.

### The Mouth.

1. He that hath a great and broad mouth is shameless, a great babbler and liar, proud to an excess, and ever abounding in quarrelsome words.

2. A small mouth denotes a Person Peaceable and faithful.

3. Those that have the lips small and thin, are great talkers and railers, and given to deceit and falsehood.

4. Lips that are a little thick, and well coloured, are faithful, and given to virtue; and those who have the lips pleasantly pouting, are reckoned one of Venus's greatest beauties.

5. Those that have one lip thicker than the other, are of little understanding, slow to comprehend, and rather guilty of folly than wisdom.

### The Ears.

1. Great, big, broad ears, signify a simple man, of no understanding; sluggish, slothful, and of an ill memory.

2. Small ears denote a good understanding; but very small ears signify nothing but mischief.

3. Those that have them long and thin, are bold, impudent, unlearned, gluttons, and whore-masters, and very proud in general.

4. Those that have them well proportioned, and neither too small nor too large, are persons of good understanding, wise, discreet, honest, shamefaced, and courageous.

### The Face in general.

1. The face that is round, plump, and ruddy, shews the person to be of an agreeable temper, well deserving of friendship, and faithful in love.

2. A face with very prominent cheekbones, thin and long visage, shews a restless disposition, and rarely satisfied with anything.

3. A face naturally pale, denotes the person very amorous.

4. Blue eyes are mostly to be depended on for fidelity, though there is never a rule without an exception, for many blue-eyed are capable of bad deeds.

5. Dark eyes are generally suspicious, artful, and prone to deceit.

6. A very fair person is in general, indifferent proud, neglectful to please, and though amorous, is too haughty to let the world believe they would think it worth the trouble of appearing agreeable.

7. A countenance tolerably fair, cheerful, and well-formed, with dark brown hair, is most to be depended on for fidelity.

## MOLES

———

These are little marks on the skin, although they, appear to be the effect of chance or accident, and might easily pass with the unthinking for things of no moment, are nevertheless of the utmost consequence, since front their colour, situation, size, and figure, may be accurately gathered, the temper of, and the events that will happen to the person bearing
them.

1. *A Mole on the wrist*, or between that and the finger ends, shews the person to be of an ingenious and industrious turn, faithful in his engagements, amorous and constant in his affections, rather of a saving disposition, with a great degree of sobriety and regularity in his dealings.
2. *A Mole between the elbow and the wrist*, shews a placid and cheerful disposition, industry, and & love of reading, particularly books of science.
3. *A Mole near either elbow*, shews a restless and. Unsteady disposition, with a great desire of travelling—much discontented in the marriage state, and of an idle turn.
4. *A Mole on the right or left arm*, shews courageous disposition, great fortitude, resolution, industry, and conjugal felicity.
5. *A Mole on the left shoulder*, shews a person of a quarrelsome and unruly disposition, always inclined to dispute for trifles, rather indolent, but much inclined to the pleasures of love, and faithful to

the conjugal vows.

6. *A Mole on the right shoulder*, shews a person of a prudent and discreet temper, one possessed of much wisdom, given to great secrecy, very industrious, but not very amorous, yet faithful to the conjugal ties.

7. *A Mole on the loins*, shews industry and honesty, an amorous disposition, with great vigour, courage, and fidelity.8. A Mole on the hip, shews that the person will have many children.

8. *A Mole on the right thigh*, shews that the person will become rich, and have good luck in marriage.

9. *A Mole on the left thigh*, denotes that the person suffers ranch by poverty and want of friends, as also by the enmity and injustice of others.

10. *A Mole on the right knee*, portends that the person will be rash, inconsiderate, and hasty.

11. *A Mole on the left knee*, shews a hasty and passionate disposition, with an inconsiderate turn.

12. *A Mole on either leg*, shews that the person is indolent, and indifferent as to what happens.

13. *A Mole on either ankle*, denotes a man to be inclined to effeminacy and elegance of dress; a woman to be courageous, active, and industrious.

14. *A Mole on either foot*, forbodes sudden illness, or unexpected misfortune.

15. *A Mole that stands on the tight side of the forehead or right temple*, signifies that the person will arrive to sudden wealth and honour.

16. *A Mole on the right eyebrow,* announces speedy marriage; and that the person to whom you will be married, will possess money, amiable qualities, and a fortune.

17. *A Mole on the outside corner of either eye*, denotes the person to be of a steady, sober, and sedate disposition; but will be liable to a violent death.

18. *A Mole on either cheek*, signifies that the person never shall rise above mediocrity in point of fortune, though at the same time he will never sink to real poverty.

19. *A Mole on both cheeks* denotes the person will know a deal of trouble, losses, and crosses, but at
last arrive to be a great tradesman and will gain great riches; will

be a very public character; and
also fond of rural scenes.

20. *A Mole on the lip*, cither upper or lower, prevents the person to be fond of delicate things, and very much given to the pleasures of love, in which he or she will be successful.

21. *A Mole on the side of the neck*, shews that the person will narrowly escape suffocation but afterwards rise to great consideration by an unexpected legacy or inheritance.

22. *A Mole on the throat*, denotes that the person shall become rich by marriage.

23. *A Mole on the bosom*, portends mediocrity of health and fortune.

24. *A Mole under the left breast over the heart*, forehews that man will be of a warm disposition, unsettled in mind, fond of rambling, and light in his conduct; in woman, it shews sincerity in love, quick conception, and easy to travel in childbirth.

25. *A. Mole on the belly* denotes the person to be addicted to sloth and gluttony; selfish in almost all articles, and seldom inclined to be nice or careful in point of dress.

26. *A Mole situated in those recesses* which modesty conceals from view, as not to admit of being discovered but by another: and yet to have a Mole so placed is the most fortunate for them.

## PALMISTRY.

---

The Palms of the hands contain a great variety of lines running in different directions, every one of which bears a certain relation to the events of a person's life: and from them, with the most infallible certainty, can be told every circumstance that will happen to anyone, by observing them properly.

It is therefore recommended to pay a strict attention to this object, as by that means you will undoubtedly gain very excellent knowledge for your pains and first is given the names of the several lines as they hold their places, and then particularize their qualities.

*There are five principal lines in hand:*
The Line of Life, or Life Line as it is here called.
The Line of Death.
The Table Line
The Girdle of Venus.
The Line of Fortune.


And besides these there are other Lines, as the *Line of Saturn*; the Liver Line, and some others, but these only serve to explain the principal Lines. The chief Lines can which persons of the profession lay the greatest stress, is the *Line of Life*, or the Life Line, as it is here called, which generally takes its rise where the thumb joint plays with the: wrist on the inside; and runs in an oblique direction to the inside of the innermost joint of the forefinger.

The next is the *Line of Death* which separates the fleshy part of the hand on the little finger side, from the hollow of the band, running in various directions in different people.

The Table Line originates with the *Life Line*, at the wrist, and runs through the hollow of the hand towards the middle finger.

The *Girdle of Venus* takes its course from the extremity of the innermost joint of the little finger, and forming a curve, terminates between the fore and middle fingers.

The *Line of Fortune* strikes from behind the ball, or mount of the fore finger, across the palm and *Line of Life*, and loses itself in or near the fleshy part of the hand on the little finger side.

If the *Line of Life* is crossed by other Lines at or near the wrist, the person will meet with sickness in the beginning of life, and the degree of sickness will be proportioned to the size, length, and breadth of the intervening lines. If the *Life Line* runs fair and uninterrupted, the person will enjoy good health; and according to its length towards the outside of the fore finger, you may judge if the person will live long, as the longer the Line the longer the Life.

If the *Line of Death* is short, and runs even, without being broken or divided, it shews that the person will enjoy a good length of days, and not be subject to many maladies; but if it is interrupted, it evidently shews that the person's life will be endangered by illness, but by the care of Providence will recover.

When the Table Line is broad, strong, and well-marked, it shews the person to be of a sound constitution, and a peaceable contented mind: if it is broken, it shews for every break a violent interruption to happiness ; if these breaks happen towards the part next the wrist, he will be crossed in love, and either be disappointed in the person he has fixed his affections on, or be saddled with a person of a disobliging temper, and a most audacious and abusive tongue.

*The Girdle of Venus*, when it goes on fair and well-marked, shews that the person will be prosperous in love, fair in his dealings with the fair sex, and be sincerely-beloved; he will obtain a partner for life of a fortune equal to his own, sweet tempered, faithful, and affectionate; but if it is interrupted at its beginning near the little finger, he will meet with early disappointments in love; if towards the middle of the line, he will rum his health, and inure his fortune with lewd prostitutes; if near the end, he will be foolishly amorous in his old age, still expecting to gain the heart of a woman, but never will obtain it.

*The Line of Fortune*, by its approach to tire *Girdle of Venus*, shews that there is a strong kindred between them, and their distance at their two extremities clearly point out that love is inconsistent with childhood, and old age; yet in those where the cross line approach from the one to the other near the ends, prove that the persons were, or will be susceptible of love in childhood; or old age.

If the hollow palm of the hand: which some call the *Plain of Mars*, is full of cross lines running into' each other, the person will be of a

215

humoursome, uneven, and testy temper, jealous and hasty, quarrel-
some and fighting, and endeavouring to set others by the ears; he will meet with very frequent, misfortunes, and bear them very uneasily; whereas, if the hollow or palm of the hand has none but the unavoidable lines, that is to say, those that must unavoidably pass through it, he will be of a sweet and amiable disposition, full of sensibility, gratitude, and love, faithful, benevolent, and kind ; and though subject to losses, crosses, and disappointments, will hear them with an even and agreeable temper; from this part chiefly, it is recommended to persons to choose their companions for life, either for friendship or marriage.

The mount or ball of the thumb, bears a particular analogy to the events of a person's life, with I respect to disputes, quarrels and lawsuits; if this mount has many long strait lines reaching from the thumb to the *Line of Life*, they show that the person will have several personal encounters; either with hands, clubs, pistols or swords; but if the lines are curved and crooked, they will indicate lawsuits, and according to the degree of crookedness, they will be long or short but if these lines end in a straight direction towards the line of life, they will end prosperously, whether encounter or law-suits if otherwise, they will be attended with an unfavourable issue; the nearer to the line of life these lines begin, the later in a person's life the quarrels or law-suits will take place; and the nearer to the line of life they end, the later in life they will terminate.


## TO TELL FORTUNES BY THE GROUNDS OF A COFFEE-CUP


*Directions to pour out the Coffee-grounds.*
Pour the grounds of coffee in a white cup, shake them well about in it, so that their particles may over the surface of the whole cup; then reverse it into the saucer, that superfluous parts may be drained, and the figures required for fortune-telling performed. The person that acts the fortune-teller must bend their thoughts upon the person that wishes their fortune told, and upon their rank and professions, in order to give plausibility to their predictions. It is not

to be expected upon taking up the cup, that the figures will be accurately represented as they are in the pack, and it is quite sufficient if they bear some resemblance to any of the following emblems.

### The Roads.

Or serpentine lines, indicate ways; if they are covered with clouds, they are said to be infallible marks either of past or future reverses. If they appear clear and serene, they are a sure token of some fortunate chance near at hand: encompassed with very many dots, they signify an accidental gain of money, likewise long life.

### The Ring.

I Signifies marriage; if a letter is near it, it denotes to the person that has his fortune told, the initial of the name of the pasty to be married. Likewise, if the ring is in the cleat, it portends happy and lucrative friendship. Surrounded with clouds, designs that the person is to use precaution in friendship he is about to contract. If the ring appears at the bottom of the cup, it forebodes an entire separation from the beloved object.

### The Leaf of Clover.

Is as well here as in common life, a lucky sign, Its different position in the cup alone makes the diference; because if it is on the top, it shews that it signifies a considerable estate left to the party by some rich relation; in the same manner at the bottom, it shews that the deceased is not so nearly elated to the consulting party.

### The Star

Denotes happiness if in the clear, and at the top of the cup; clouded, or in the thick, it signifies long life, though exposed to various vicissitudes and troubles. If ants are about it, it foretells good fortune, wealth, high respectability, &c. Several stars denote so many good and happy children; but surrounded with dashes, shews that your children will cause you grief and vexation in your old age, and

that you ought to prevent it by giving them a good education in time.


### The Dog.
Being at all times the emblem of fidelity or envy, has also a two-fold meaning here. At the top, in the clear, it signifies true and faithful friends; but if his image be surrounded with clouds or dashes,
it shews that those whom you take for your friends are not to be depended on; but if the dog be at the bottom of the cup, you have to dread the effects of extreme envy or jealousy.


### The Lily.
If this emblem be at the top, or in the middle of the cup, it signifies that the consulting party either has or will have a virtuous spouse; if it be at the bottom, it denotes quite the reverse. In the clear, the lily further betokens long and happy life; if clouded, or in the thick, it portends trouble and vexation, especially on the part of one's relation.


### The Cross.
Be it one or more, it generally predicts adversities, ills position varies, and so do the circumstances. If it be at the top, and in the clear, it shews that the misfortunes of the party will soon be at an end, or that he will easily get over them; but if it appears
in the middle, or at the bottom in the thick; the party must expect many severe trials: if it a pear with dots, either in the clear or in the thick it promises a speedy change of one's sorrow.


### The Clouds.
If they be more light than dark, you may expect a good result from your hopes; but if they are black, you may give it up. Surrounded with dots they imply success in trade, and' in all your undertakings; but the brighter they are, the greater will be your happiness.

218

### The Sun.
An emblem of the greatest luck and happiness if in toe clear; but in the thick it bodes a great deal of sadness; surrounded by dots or dashes denotes that an alteration will easily take place.

### The Moon.
If it appears in the clear, it denotes high honours in the dark, or thick part, it implies sadness, which will, however, pass without great prejudice. But if it be at the bottom of the cup, the consulting party will be very fortunate both by water and land.

### Mountain.
If it represents only one mountain, it indicate the favour of people of high rank, but several of them, especially in the thick, are signs of powerful enemies; in the clear, they signify the contrary, or friends in high life, who are endeavouring to premote the consulting party.

### The Tree.
One tree only, be it in the clear or thick part points out lasting good health; several trees denotes that your wish will be accomplished.

### The Child.
In the clear part, it bespeaks innocent intercourse between the consultor and another person; in the thick part, excesses in love matters, attended with great expenses: at the bottom of the cup it denote the consequences of libidinous amours, and a very destructive end.

## *The true method of telling your Fortune, by* CARDS.

TAKE a pack of [playing] Cards, and pick Six out of each sort, viz. the 8, 9, 10, Knave, King & Queen, else being the most Prophetic Cards in the Pack, let the Person whose Fortune is to be learned be
blindfolded. This done, let the Cards be shuffled, and the whole dealt out singly on the table, with their faces downwards. The bandage being then taken off the eyes of the blinded person; he or she must take up any ore of the Cards; when, by explaining the following Rules, the true Fortune maybe known. The W. at the beginning of each stanza, stands for Woman, and M. for Man.

### *Eight of Diamonds.*
*W.*—Dear miss you seem mighty uneasy and look on the Cards with a frown: the conjuror wants not to tease ye, But all the bad fortune's your own. You are doom'd for to live an old maid, ma'am, and never blest with your man; But have courage, and be net afraid, ma'am,
You'll give us the lie if you can.

*M.*—To wander thro' your native fields, on rural pleasure bent; This Card to you that blessing yields,O take it as 'twas meant. Cheerful improve each fleeting hour,Alas! they fly full fast; do all the good within your power and never dread the last.

### Nine of Diamonds.

*W.*-The English girl who draws this Card, will have no cause to fret her;Yet if she thinks her fortune hard, She'll struggle for a better: But if the same Card comes again. Old Scotland's curse attends her and she may scratch, auld scratch again, till grease and brimstone mends her.

*M.*—111 fate betide the wretched man, to whom this Card shall fall;
His race on earth will soon be ran, his happiness but small. Disloyalty shall stain his fame, his days be mark'd with strife, Newgate shall record his name, and Tyburn end this life.

### Ten of Diamonds.

*W.*—Peace and plenty will attend you. if I happen to befriend you: Children ten your lot will be, a single one, and three times three; But if twins you'll chance to have, you'll surely find an early grave.
*M.*—Whate'er his endeavours a man who gets this Shall a bachelor be all his life; He never shall taste of the conjugal bliss, nor ever be curs'd with a wife.

### The Knave of Diamonds.

*W.*—Madam, your fortune's mighty queer, The conjuror discovers; to fools you'll lend a listening ear and knaves will be your lovers.
*M*—In Venus's wars, on London plains, he'll spend his early youth; The knave of diamonds if he gains;Nay, never doubt the truth. To prove this bold assertion just, your surgeon's bill produce; expose your nose, and own you must, That nose unfit for use.

### Queen of Diamonds.

*W.*—If this queen to an amorous widow shall come, who has lately interr'd a good man, for a husband again she will quickly make room, and plague him as much as she can't but let her beware how she trifles with him. Tho' she fool'd with the sot that's departed; for in that case most surely her hide he will trim, till her ladyship dies broken hearted.

*M.* —-The married man that draws this card, Will soon a cuckold be

Nor let him think his fortune hard in so much company. For out of twenty married pair, search all the country through, nineteen at feast the horns must wear, and pray why should not you.

### King of Diamonds.

*W.*—Alas! poor girl, though I lament your fate, I cannot save you from a husband's hate; a tyrant Lord will rule you thro' your life, and make you curse the wretched name of wife.

*M*—To Lords and great people frequenting the court, this card will most auspicious prove. To the closets of princes, they'll freely resort and be rich in their sovereign's love. Yet in those of low rank no good it portends but oppression and hardship forerun; unkind will be all their relations and friend, ungrateful their daughters and sons.

### Eight- of Clubs.

*W.*—Little peevish, crabbed elf, fond of no one but herself, cross, and still for trifles striving, with her truly there's no living.

*M.*—Tho' honest you look & you speak a man fair, yet you know you're a rascal in grain; for sixpence your soul to the devil you'll swear but he'll send such a thief back again.

### Nine of Clubs.

*W.*—If this card you shall draw, O return it again be quick, ma'am, to take my advice; For its only production are trouble and pain And I hope you will not draw it twice. But such your misfortune, I've nothing to say to assist you is out of my power, the stars are enacting the devil to pay and the play-house is open'd at four. Af—Fu I well I foresaw that the devil to pay, would harass each young female elf, and see, my dear ladies, to help on the play; that here comes the devil himself.

### Ten of Clubs.

*W.*—'Tis not your fortune, wit, or birth. Can the day of death defer; you'll soon return to parent earth, and mix your lovely dust with her. This will prove a mourning card, and drown in tears the fairest face,

But her fate is no ways hard, the lot of all the human race.

*M.*—Bad luck to a woman is good to man, and it happens so often through life; let the man who draws this deny it if he car for he quickly shall bury his wife.

### Knave of Clubs.

*W.*—Though much I pity your sad fate, yet does my pity come too late

To ward off fortune's rubs; though you the queen of hearts should prove, a surly brute shall gain your love, a very knave of clubs.

*M.* —Whatever you presume to say, the world will talk a different way. ere well your words transpire: Ask you, good sir, the reason why,

You'll know my answer is no lie, no man believes a liar.

### Queen of Clubs.

*W.*—Ah, Madam, too well you love kissing I find. my reason I scarcely need tell ye. for while you draw this, by a fortune unkind, your neighbours regard your big belly.

*M.*—And here comes the hero that get the Gray brat (cloak), lord, sir, you your blushes may spare, for the world too well knows what you have been at but dispel the poor lass's despair.

### King of Clubs.

*W.*—This, the last, a generous card, will the first of blessings prove: be but true, nor doubt reward, in a husband's faithful love.

*M.*—Of clubs the king, to you who ill portends, friendly yourself, you'll meet with many friends.

### Eight of Hearts.

*W.*—In the days of your courtship you'll bill like a dove, but when age shall advance you'll drink hard. both kissing and tippling you'll show that you love.If your fortune shall send you this card.

*M.*—A numerous family falls to the man, whose fortune* shall give him this card; so let him maintain 'em as well as he can, nor grumble, or think his case hard.

### Nine of Hearts.
*W.*—A coach and six horses will fall to the main, whose first chance this card shall obtain but if 'tis her second, I'm greatly afraid. She must come to plain walking again.
*M.*—-The man however great or grand, who draws the nine of hearts. For aught that I can understand, is one of shallow parts.

### Ten of Hearts.
*W.*—Deck'd with ev'ry female grace. Sweet in person, mind, and face, then a mother soon shall be with thy lovely progeny.
*M.*—Ten children you'll have, if this card you get, and i think you will wish for no more; If you do try again, 'tis your fate. You cannot have less than a score.

### Knave of Hearts.
*W.*—This rascally knave will your fortune cofound. Except special care you shall take; for while scores of young lovers your step shall surround, you'll accept of a doting old rake.
*M.*—Nothing can ever save the man who draws this cursed card;
A vixen will his heart trepan:
Alas! his case is hard.

### Queen of Hearts.
*W.*—-The queen of Love will favour, who draws the queen of hearts, and many a blessing will confer; the fruit of female hearts.

*M.*—From girl to girl you'll often range, never with one content;
But yet the oftener you shall change, the oftener you'll repent.

### King of Hearts.

*W.*—If this you draw, condemn'd throughout your life, a peevish maiden, and a vixen wife; unchaste while married, and a widow wan-
ton; all this you'll be, and more could I descant on.
*M.*—Your fortune can't be mighty good, for a vile whore will please you, who never would do what she should, but make your life uneasy.

### Eight of Spades.

*W.*—If youthful lasses draw the eight of spades. they'll toy away their time with amorous blades,
*M.*—If a doctor, lawyer, quaker, priest; should fix on this card but his hand. The conjuror swears, and he swears 'tis net, that some rogues will be found in the land.

### Nine of Spades.

*W*—The lass who gets this unlucky, hated card, a shrivell'd maid shall die, which you think is hard.
*M.*—How often our fortunes by opposites go; what brings bliss to a man, to a woman brings woe.

### Ten of Spades.

*W.*—Pretty ladies, young and fair,
Always young and debonair, life with you will sweetly glide, and you will be a happy bride.
*M.*—You the happy man will prove.
Who obtains the lady's love.

### Knave of Spades.

*W.*—If this knave you should obtain, put him in the pack again;
For the rascal brings all kinds of news, such as you must never chase.
*M.*—Of all the cards throughout the pack, no worse to man can

come;
His wife will stun him with her clack, and make him hate his home.

### *Queen of Spades.*

*W.*— An elegant behaviour makes the lass, through whose fair hand this card shall pas'

*M.*—The rule of contrarieties we see, of man, the most unhappy he who this ill-fated card shall take, is wife will be a perfect rake.

### *King of Spades.*

*W.*—The ladies of fashion this card who obtain, in vain on the court may attend his Majesty's favours they never will gain, nor Sad at St. James's a friend.

*M.*—But a contrary fate on the man will attend, his king will some favours bestow; the poor and the wretched he'll often befriend and cherish the children of woe.

# FINIS

226

# BIBLIOGRAPHY

Abercromby, John; '*Traditions, Customs and Superstitions of the Lewis*', Folklore Vol.6, No.2. Taylor & Francis, Ltd (1895)

Ashliman, D.L; Magic Books: legends from Northern Europe (2003-2021) [online source] available at: https://www.pitt.edu/~dash/magicbook.html

Black, PhD. George. F; *County Folk-lore Vol. III: Orkney and Shetland Islands,* Taylor & Francis, Ltd. on behalf of Folklore Enterprises, Ltd.(1903)

Black, PhD. George. F; *Witchcraft in Scotland: A Calendar of cases of witchcraft in Scotland, 1510-1727*, Erfimid William Ronghead. W. S. (1937)

Black, William George, '*Charms and Spells at Gretna*', Folk-Lore Journal Volume VI (1888)

Cameron, Isabel; *Highland Chapbook*, Mackay Stirling (1928)

Campbell, John Gregorson, 1836-1891.; Ed. Black, Ronald.; *The Gaelic otherworld* : John Gregorson Campbell's *Superstitions of the Highlands & Islands of Scotland and Witchcraft & second sight in the Highlands & Islands* / edited with commentary by Ronald Black. Edinburgh, Birlinn (2005)

Clerk, Dr. A.; "*Notes on Ancient Gaelic Medicine* (1890)", "Transactions of the Gaelic Society of Glasgow Volume I, 1887-91"

Chambers, Robert; *The Popular Rhymes of Scotland: With Illustrations, Chiefly Collected from Oral Sources*. W. Hunter, 1826

Carmichael, Alexander, Ed. James Carmichael Watson; *The Carmina Gadelica Vols.1-3*, T. and A. Constable, Edinburgh (1832–1912)

Dalydell, John Graham; '*The Darker Superstitions of Scotland*', Richard Griffins & co.; Thomas Tegg and Son, London (1834)

Davies, Owen; *A Comparative Perspective on Scottish Cunning-Folk and Charmers*, Witchcraft and Belief in Early Modern Scotland, J. Goodare, L. Martin & J. Miller, Palgrave Macmillian Uk (12/04/2007)

Davies, Owen, *Grimoires: A History of Magic Books*, Oxford University Press, (01/12/2010)

Davies, Owen; *Popular Magic: Cunning-folk in English History*, Hambledon Continuum; New Ed edition (01/06/2007)

Fielding, Penny; *black books: sedition, circulation, and the lay of the last minstrel* [Article], Baltimore, Vol.81, Iss, (spring, 2014)

Guthrie, Ellen Emma, '*Old Scottish Customs: Local and General*', London: Hamilton, Adams & co. Thomas D. Morison (Glasgow 1885)

Goodare, Julian, Lauren Martin and Joyce Miller; '*Witchcraft and Belief in Early Modern Scortland*', Palgrave Macmillian (2008)

Howard, Michael; '*Scottish Witches and Warlock's*, Witchcraft of the British Isles Series Book III, Three Hands Press (2013)

Johnson, Dr. Thomas K.; *Svartkonstböcker: A Compendium of the Swedish Black Art Book Tradition*, Revelore Press (2019)

Kerr, Cathel "*Fishermen and Superstition*", The Celtic Magazine Vol. XIII 1887-88

Kirk, Robert and Andrew Lang; '*The Secret Commonwealth of Elves, Fauns and Fairies*', London: David Nutt, In the Strand (1893)

Rustad, Mary. S; *The Black Books of Elverum*, Galde Press, Inc (2009)

Simpkins, John Ewart; *County Folk-lore Vol.VII: Fife, Clackmannan and Kinross-shires*, Taylor & Francis, Ltd. on behalf of Folklore Enterprises, Ltd.(1914)

Mackenzie, William; '*Gaelic Incantations, Charms and Blessing of the Hebrides: with translations, and parallel illustrations from Irish, Manx, Norse and other superstitions*', The Northern Counties Newspaper and Printing and Publishing Company limited (Inverness 1895)

Marwick, Ernest W., '*The Folklore of Orkney and Shetland*', B.T Batsford LTD (London 1975)

Lawless, Sarah Anne; '*Horse and Hattock: The Origins of the Witch's chant*', The Witch of Forest Grove. [online source] Available at: https://www.scribd.com/document/163885180/By-Horse-and-Hattock-The-Origin-of-the-Witches-Chant

MacBain, Alexander; '*Incantations and Magic Rhymes*', Highland Monthly volume III (1891-92)

Maclagan, R. C.; 'Notes on Folklore Objects Collected in Argyleshire', Folklore, 6:2, 144-161 (1895)

McNeill, F. Marian; The Silver Bough vol. I: Scottish Folklore and Folk-belief, William MacLellan (1977)

McPherson, J. M; Primitive Beliefs in the North-East of Scotland, Longmanas, Green and co. London (1929)

Martin, Martin: 'A Description of the Western Islands of Scotland', London: Printed for Andrew Bell, at the Cross-Keys and Bible, in Cornhill, near Stocks-Market (1703)

Masson, Donald; 'Notes from the North highlands', The Archaeological Review. A Journal Of Historic And Prehistoric Antiquities, Vol IV. (August 1889 – January 1890)

Page, Sophie; Spellbound: Magic, Ritual and Witchcraft, Ashmolean Museum Publications; 01 edition (29 Aug. 2018)

Pitcairn, Robert; Ancient Criminal Trials in Scotland (Edinburgh 1833)

Roper, Jonathan Roper. Ed; 'Charms, Charmers and Charming: International Research on Verbal Magic', Palgrave Macmillian (Hampshire 2009)

Wilby, Emma; 'We mey shoot them dead at our pleasur': Isobel Gowdie, Elf Arrows and Dark Shamanism', Ed. Julian Goodare; Scottish Witches and Witch-hunters, Palgrave macmillian (2013)

Wilby, Emma; Visions of Isobel Gowdie: Magic, Shamanism and Witchcraft in Seventeenth-Century Scotland, Sussex Academic Press; New Ed edition (1 Jun. 2010)

## Recommended Books

Svartkonstböker: A Compendium of the Swedish Black Art Book Tradition by Dr. Thomas K. Johnson

The Wicked Shall Declay: Charms, Spells & Witchcraft of Old Britain by A.D Mercer

The British Book of Spells and Charms by Graham King

The Visions of Isobel Gowdie: Magic, Shamanism and Witchcraft in Seventeenth-Century Scotland by Emma Wilby

Healing Threads: Traditional Medicines of the Highlands and Lowlands by Mary Beith

*Scottish Witches and Warlocks* by Michael Howard

*The Folklore of the Scottish Highlands* by Ann Ross

## Online resources

The Survey of Scottish Witchcraft- http://www.shca.ed.ac.uk/Research/witches//

Electric Scotland: history and culture of Scotland and the Scots at home and abroad- https://electricscotland.com/

> ➢ For the *Carmina Gadelica* volumes 1-4 online: https://www.electricscotland.com/books/pdf/carmina.htm

Virtual Hebrides: Images from the western isles- https://www.virtualheb.co.uk/

Stuart McHardy: A Lad o Pairts Speaks- 'The devil in isobel Gowdie'- https://stuartmchardy.wordpress.com/2013/04/02/isobel-gowdie/

The National Library of Scotland- https://www.nls.uk/

Survey of Scottish witchcraft (SSW 1563-1736)- http://www.shca.ed.ac.uk/Research/witches//

Orknejar: *The history of the Orkney Islands*- http://www.orkneyjar.com/

Orkney Archive: *Get dusty*- http://orkneyarchive.blogspot.com/

Tobar an Dualchais/Kist o Riches- https://www.tobarandualchais.co.uk/

DSL- Dictionaries of the Scots Language at https://dsl.ac.uk/

LearnGaelic- https://learngaelic.scot/dictionary/

Sacred Texts: Celtic- https://www.sacred-texts.com/neu/celt/index.htm

Printed in Great Britain
by Amazon

65853282R00139